Credit and Collections

Credit and Collections:
A Business Perspective

By

Michelle Dunn

CAMBRIDGE
SCHOLARS
PUBLISHING

Credit and Collections: A Business Perspective,
by Michelle Dunn

This book first published 2013

Cambridge Scholars Publishing

12 Back Chapman Street, Newcastle upon Tyne, NE6 2XX, UK

British Library Cataloguing in Publication Data
A catalogue record for this book is available from the British Library

ISBN (10): 1-4438-4369-5, ISBN (13): 978-1-4438-4369-0

TABLE OF CONTENTS

FOREWORD

I was in elementary school when one of my teachers gave me a certificate that stated I was the most likely in my class to be a successful business woman.

I have been an entrepreneur my entire life, I started with raking leaves, shoveling snow, picking blueberries by the lake then going door to door and selling them, picking up old neighbors newspapers in my wagon and getting rid of them, (though many times I would bring them home and read through them and cut out pictures and cartoons for collages on my bedroom wall). I would make crafts and sell them on the street, during the gas crisis in the 70s the line from the gas station at the end of my road traveled way past my house so I set up a lemonade stand and enlisted my brothers to deliver cups of lemonade to people waiting in their hot cars for their turn at the pump.

After some bumps in the road I eventually was able to attend a local community college while working three jobs. I eventually was able to cut back to two jobs, one being an administrative assistant which gave me experience and knowledge about working in an office and how it all comes together. I have had many jobs in credit, mostly as a credit manager and I always collected more money than any other credit managers had before me. Because of this, I normally would work myself out of a job. When I was getting divorced and traveling 2 hours to one of my credit manager jobs, I decided to start my own collection agency.

My experience includes working in accounting, working as an accounts receivable clerk, credit manager and third party collector and agency owner. I also started my own Credit & Collections discussion group which still has thousands of members, some having been members for over 18 years.

To share my knowledge about being an effective collector I have written many books on the subject, most of them part of my Collecting Money Series and others for major publishers. Many of my books are now also available for Kindle or the Kindle App so anyone can read them on their computer, Kindle, phone, iPad or any electronic device.

CHAPTER ONE

WHY BUSINESSES NEED A CREDIT MANAGEMENT PLAN

The sale is not complete until you get paid

As a business owner, your business is one of many that allow consumers to use goods or services immediately and pay for them later. While extending credit like this increases your gross sales, it also puts your business at risk of some losses due to non-payment. You don't have to accept excessive bad debt losses as a part of doing business. Learning how to establish and maintain effective credit procedures and management plans over cash flow are not that hard and it will help you reduce your bad debt losses.

The most important benefit you can gain from improving your cash flow and collection activities is improved and increased cash flow, more time to focus on your business and success. Without improving cash flow and collection procedures, businesses risk their own success. If you do not get paid on time and as agreed you may not have the money to pay your own bills which will hurt your credit with vendors, banks and suppliers. By improving your cash flow your business can be successful, make more sales and increase the bottom line. When a customer pays you late, even just 10 days, you are losing your profit, so this is very important to your business.

In my experience businesses are always keeping bad financial records or none at all. This contributes to their downfall, and so it is very important for businesses to keep up and follow up with their financial situation. When a business doesn't follow up with their financials, they are saying that they are not serious about their cash flow and if they are not serious about their cash, their customers will not be either. Setting a precedent that shows your employees and customers that you are serious about your business and its cash lets them know that you are watching accounts, you are serious about your terms, and how you want to be paid and you will not put up with non-payment or late payments without noticing and following up with the customer to find out where their payment or money is. Not following up with customers or watching accounts leads to cash flow problems and in some cases those businesses then cannot pay their own bills, affecting their business credit, how they do business, their employees' jobs and how long they may be able to stay in business.

If you don't show your customers or potential customers that you are in business to make money and that you will be keeping track of your cash flow they will see that it is not something you monitor and everyone will want to do business with you. If on the other hand, every customer has to fill out and sign a credit application or contract and you check their references for a guide on how much credit you are going to extend to customers based on their credit worthiness, you send a message to your customers and employees. That message is that you are not fooling around, you are in business to make money and you are serious about getting paid. This deters customers from late or non-payment; they will pay your bill before another company's invoice that doesn't take any steps to limit their credit risk. I find this has been similar to raising children, once they know what they can get away with; they will try to take advantage of that and more. It is up to you as the business owner or credit manager to take the responsibility to train or teach your new and existing customers how you want to get paid, when you want to get paid and what is going to happen if you are not paid according to your set terms. This keeps your business in charge of your cash flow instead of allowing the customer to be in charge of your cash.

Having a credit policy or credit management plan has always been an important part of every business and when "easy credit" entered the picture it was confusing to many people who legitimately offered credit terms. Why were lenders trying to entice consumers who had little or no credit, or even consumers with bad credit to borrow money from them? Lenders could make more money by lending money or extending credit to people who could not afford it and who had bad credit in the first place. You may ask me how that affects your business or its credit. This affects our economy and is creating many more new difficulties for borrowing money for many homeowners and companies that have bad credit and in some cases where they have "passable" credit and even some money to put down. Quite a change from the last few years where you could get credit with "No Credit Check" or with "Bad Credit" or "No Credit". This credit crisis began with a focus on the subprime mortgage industry and has now spread into highly leveraged companies and we are still in the midst of a very weak market in terms of credit that reaches globally.

Since you are reading this book you are looking for answers or help to maintain good customers' relations and smooth payment processes and cash flow. As a credit manager or the owner of a business you should be able to answer the following questions or at least know how to find these answers if you want an effective credit management plan.

1. How do debt and credit affect my business?
2. Exactly what is my credit policy?
3. What makes a successful credit policy?
4. What is credit risk?
5. How do I turn prospects into credit approved customers?
6. How can I maximize my cash flow?
7. How do I handle customer deductions?
8. How do I handle customer excuses for late payments?
9. Why would I use a third party collection agency?

Your credit management plan should answer each of those questions; you and your employees should be able to flip through your credit policy to find out what steps to take in each of those instances. This book can help you create a plan that answers those questions and gives you a guideline and steps to take in each scenario, helping your cash flow smoothly and avoiding much bad debt and frustration.

Many business owners worry about how the economy will affect their business. As a business owner you need to understand the economy enough to know that your business will be affected before a recession or any hard times actually hit and you must take preventative steps in order to avoid problems when and if it does hit hard.

One thing you can do is make sure that forecasting is something you do for your business or ask your accountant to help you with this. Look for growth in real wages, which drives consumer spending, and which accounts for more than 2/3 of the US economy. Consumer spending is a huge indicator of what is happening and it also drives corporate profits which in turn affect the stock market. Look for changes in the economy that will affect your business and remember every business is affected differently and at different times during the cycle of a recession, or down turn.

Keeping up to date on foreclosures happening in your area and the areas you may sell services or products to is crucial to your business. You can make sure your business is protected by going over all of your accounts that you extend credit to, make sure they are in good standing and up to date on all invoices. If you have signed credit applications and are authorized to pull credit reports and/or check with banks and vendors on someone's payment history, now is the time to re-evaluate each customer's credit and credit limits. Look for things such as late or slower arriving payments, change or loss of a job, changes in incomes, change of address, and divorce. Take immediate action if a customer's mail is returned and/or if the phone is disconnected. Many times when the economy suffers people lose their jobs, their relationships suffer, and they may move to cheaper housing or lose their vehicles. All of these things are factors that lead to your bill not being paid and can sometimes end in bankruptcy. The three steps you can take to help you in this situation are:

1. Review your accounts receivables weekly or at least monthly
2. Stay motivated by trying to collect as much past due money as possible
3. Stay focused; don't let customer excuses veer you off track

I know I have talked about cash flow as the main reason why business need a credit management plan but you also need a plan to protect your business credit. Banks want to see your finances which can include your taxes, bank statements and your cash activity with vendors and throughout your business. This helps them to see how much money you have, how you are using it and it helps them determine how much to lend to you.

Your credit management plan helps you in this situation because it includes your cash flow mission, purpose, how you will be paid, when you will be paid and what you will do if a customer doesn't pay you on time or in full. This lets the bank or investor know that you have a plan in place and are in control of your money and shows them how you will get the money you need to pay them back. Your credit management plan is the outline of your cash, how you will get it, how you will keep it and how you will continue to get more.

Every business needs a credit management plan in order to keep the cash flowing through their business. You have to know how to recognize that an account may have a problem paying you before it becomes a problem. Some of the ways you can recognize that you might run into a problem is that you may be making sales but don't have the money to pay your own bills on time or early, or when your customers are past due and are not responding to your collection efforts but continue to place orders and pay more slowly, and a big sign is when you receive any bad checks from any customer. In view of this, you should know how and when you want to be paid, what you will do when someone doesn't pay you on time or in full, and you should know what steps you will take if you receive a bad check from anyone. I want to give you some steps to help you accomplish those goals so that you can be successful.

You should have credit applications ready to go for your first customer. Print them off the internet or buy some with carbon at an office supply store. You can also have them printed with your logo, address and phone number wherever you get your business cards and letterhead.

Have steps written out on how to handle the completed credit application. An example: Check all fields, and make sure it is signed.
Let the customer know you will give the credit application to the credit manager to be processed and he or she will contact them with the results.
Take the credit application to the credit manager who takes it from there.

Have your payment terms printed on your credit applications, invoices, statements, agreements/contracts.
This way your terms are everywhere, and eliminates the excuse "I didn't know when I had to pay"

Make sure your sales and credit departments know your credit policies and procedures and who is in charge of them.
Sales and Credit fight a silent (and sometimes not so silent!) duel about credit. Sales wants to sell more to make more commission, credit wants to limit how much credit is extended to limit credit risk.

If you begin doing these things you will be taking affirmative action to secure the success of your business. For example, these credit applications, when signed by your customer, authorizes you to check their credit history, outlines your payment terms and by signing this document they agree that they understand and will comply with your payment terms, it can also give you the ability to charge interest or late fees, to add collection or attorney fees if the account ever becomes overdue.

If you have a customer that is already past due and you are trying to collect from them, the documentation that you will need are a proof of the order, a purchase order or completed order form, a proof of delivery from your shipper, and/or a signed credit application, agreement or contract. You will also need these items when and if you place the account with a third party collection agency. When I owned my agency I was surprised at how many businesses would place past due accounts with me but would not have any paperwork to support the debt. It becomes much harder to collect a debt without any supporting paperwork and it is impossible to take them to court without documentation, so without this paperwork your resources become limited.

CHAPTER TWO

HOW TO WRITE YOUR CREDIT POLICIES

Now that you know why you need a credit policy you need to come up with one that will work for you and your business. Some things to think about when sitting down to write out your credit policy steps are what you want your credit policies to do for you and your bottom line. The purpose of your credit policy should be to accomplish any of the following objectives.

I want my credit policy to:

Provide timely notification to any of my past due customers automatically to help my business eliminate old balances left on the books.

Outline steps and procedures that will provide my customers with options when they find themselves unable to pay in full or on time.

To provide my employees the steps to take when an account has a small balance due (interest, shipping, disputed item) in some cases a company might implement a rule that they write off anything under $10.00.

To provide step by step instructions to my credit manager when checking credit and setting reasonable credit limits for customers approved for revolving credit accounts.

Give us strict guidelines to follow on how to legally collect money due to us as a result of returned checks.

Have an automated system that will send out reminders to past due customers every week or two weeks.

Include the proper legal forms so that my business can keep customer credit card or debit card numbers on file with permission to automatically charge them at the time of an order or a specified date each month.

To have specific steps in place so our credit manager knows at what point an account should be placed with a third party collection agency and written off to bad debt.

Have steps in place in the event a customer's order is held due to a past due balance, I want this to include notification to the customer and an easy payment option.

Now that you have a clear picture of what you want this policy to do for you, take a look at your business mission statement. You want to write a short concise mission statement for your credit procedures. Every business has a mission statement and you want to apply that to your credit policy to write a mission statement for your cash flow.

Your credit procedures mission policy should state what the goals for these instructions are, what the goal of these procedures are, who is responsible for all the credit decisions and functions and then the actual policies or steps. For example, your policies or what you want your credit procedures to accomplish might be:

Your payment terms and conditions
Processing new customers that want revolving credit accounts
Using credit applications to check credit worthiness
Joining a credit bureau in order to pull credit reports
Setting realistic credit limits
Dealing with any past due customers
When and how to use a collection agency

Once you know what you want your credit policy to accomplish for you, it is much easier to write out steps that can help you achieve those goals. For example, I want my credit policy to provide timely notification to any of my past due customers automatically to help my business eliminate old balances left on the books, which can be accomplished by possibly utilizing a feature within your book keeping software that send out those reminders by email or into a folder that you can print at the end of the day in order to send a hard copy reminder. If you use accounts receivable software, you should be able to print out an accounts receivable aging report specifying anything over 90 or 120 days and with a balance of under $25.00. Then you can take a look at each of those accounts and decide what action should be taken.

In my experience most business find that doing any of these things is too much work and they become overwhelmed. The hardest part about this is getting started. If you can break down what you need to do into smaller tasks and begin slowly you will do much better. Three things to remember as you write your procedures are that you want to be tough but flexible, you want to have very specific guidelines or steps to take action on, and these procedures need to be consistently enforced or else they will not work. Now let's begin writing your credit policies.

Your first item will be your payment terms and conditions. Everyone will have different payment terms based on many things, such as how often they want cash coming in, when their bills are due and what their overhead is. In your credit policy include what types of payment options you offer your customers, for example cash, checks, credit or debit cards, PayPal or anything else you offer.

Your next item will be credit limits. How do you decide what limits to impose on credit approved customers? A customer's credit limit needs to be based on what they can afford or you are setting yourself and your customer up for failure. You need to consider the prices of your items, how many or how often someone orders from you and based on their credit history how much of a credit limit will be realistic to keep them ordering and keep them paying on time.

Once you do have bad debt, what will you do about it? How can you avoid it or stop it once you have it? Decide how you will identify if something is bad debt and uncollectable and what steps you will take to get it off your books.

As you write your policies you need to understand your credit risk. Credit risk is the risk of loss due to a default on a contract, or the risk of loss due to someone not paying you as agreed. If you don't demand payment up front you are leaving yourself open to credit risk. Your credit risk is the time in between when the customer leaves with your product or receives your service and when you get paid.

Some steps you can take and include in your policies to reduce your credit risk are:

Get a signed personal guarantee
Offer month-to-month credit
Offer ship-to-ship credit
Ask for a security deposit
Get a 50% (or more) deposit on every order

I want to give you an example of a couple of different credit policies that you can use as a guide for your own policy, but also want to tell you what the six main elements of your policy should be. These are steps you will take with every new customer/order and these are the steps you want to include as part of your policy and how to manage each step within your organization.

1. Each new customer will complete a new account form.
2. Every customer will have a signed credit application on file.
3. You will check each customer's credit worthiness.
4. You will set specific credit limits for each customer.
5. You will notify the customer if they are credit approved or denied.
6. You will review credit limits every 6 months and update as needed.

Now that you know what you need to do you need to make sure you also indicate what your customers need to do. To do that make sure your credit policy also covers these six things:

1. How do customers apply for credit with you?
2. What are your late fees, interest fees, court costs or bad check fees in the instance of late or non-payment?
3. What are your payment terms and conditions?
4. What is each customer's credit limit and how do you notify them of this
5. What are the buyers' responsibilities?
6. What are the sellers' responsibilities?

As an example for you, step one will be that each new customer (and your existing customers) should all fill out a credit application that has your payment terms, late fees, interest fees, bad check or collection costs indicated on the credit application. This covers 1-3 above. Number 4 is how you will decide on a credit limit and how you notify your customers about their credit limit. This is covered in Chapter 3 in great detail but you will be able to get credit references, bank references, employment information, financial information and permission to check all these things by having your customer sign and fill out a credit application.

The buyer or your customer's responsibilities, which would be paying you on time and in full, or notifying you of a discrepancy such as a shortage, payment error or anything else that would cause them not to pay your invoice in full and on time. The seller's responsibilities, shipping times must be met, inventory must be in stock and ready to go, you might send an invoice within a certain time frame.

Here is an example of a credit policy that you can use as a guide, or fill in the blanks and use it as your own, modifying it as you use it.

Credit Policy for MY Company
Include the date – and change it each time the policy is updated

Mission
The Credit Department will offer credit to all customers that fill out and sign a credit application and are found to be credit worthy.

Goals
The Credit Department's goals are to operate with one collector per 700 accounts while keeping bad debt down to less than 2% of total sales.
All customers found to be 18 days past due will be contacted by mail.
All customers found to be 25 days past due will be contacted by phone.
Accounts over 90 days old with no payment activity in the previous 3 months will be placed with a collection agency that has been approved by the credit manager.

All credit applications will be updated and re-run every 6 months.
Letters will be sent to each customer as their application is re-run to let them know if their credit limit or status has changed in any way and why.

Responsibility
The Credit Manager has full authority over all aspects of the credit and collections functions.
The Credit Manager reports to the Chief Executive Officer, the controller, depending on your company.

Policies & Procedures
No customer will be given a line of credit without completing and signing a credit application, and having their credit checked by the credit department.
Customers' terms cannot be changed without approval of the credit manager.
No accounts may be placed with a collection agency without approval from the credit manager.
Accounts looking for a credit limit higher than $5000.00 must be approved by the Chief Executive Officer/controller.

Terms of Sale
2% 15 net 30
$25.00 fee on any returned checks.
Court costs and collection fees can be added to balances placed with a collection agency or taken to court for payment.
All other special terms or discounts must be approved by the credit manager.

A Credit Policy Checklist

Who will be your credit manager, collector or in charge of the credit department? Pick one person to be in charge of all credit applications and reports. Write that name down so you can talk to that person about this responsibility and the job and make sure they are willing to hold that responsibility. Make sure everyone knows who this person is so they can go to them about anything credit related.

Get credit applications. Where to get them: online, office supply stores, CD's or books of business letters and forms, local printing companies. Download free credit applications at http://www.MichelleDunn.com/free-from-michelle or if you have a copy of my Ultimate Credit & Collections Handbook, the check IS in the mail – you have a CD in the back of the book that has examples of different credit applications you can print out and use. If you want a copy of this book with the CD, visit www.MichelleDunn.com or amazon.com.

Get some collection letters ready. Many businesses like "series" of letters, normally starting off with a friendly reminder and gradually getting stronger as payment is not forthcoming. You can find letters online, on the CD in the back of my Ultimate Book or write your own. I also have books of collection letters available at www.MichelleDunn.com that are downloadable and you can easily add your logo, address, contact information and personal details.

Research and choose a collection agency. You want to find an agency that you are comfortable with BEFORE you need it. When choosing an agency, make sure that they are fully acquainted with the nature of the goods or services that you provide. If an agency is familiar with your industry, it will be better suited to handle complex situations that arise during collections.

Do not place accounts with more than one collection agency. Make sure that if you decide to change collection agencies, the account is only be worked on by one service.

Choosing a professional collection service to manage delinquent accounts and other related tasks is a wise decision. The agency you choose should represent your company in a responsible and professional manner; they should provide a satisfactory rate of recovery while maintaining your public image. This decision involves more than just giving your business to the lowest bidder – it requires careful consideration. Remember, that the agency you choose is a reflection of you and your business.

Consider the following qualifications and credentials when you are choosing a collection agency:

Is the agency a member of a national trade association? Membership is an indication of professional integrity.

Does the agency belong to a local Chamber of Commerce?

Does the agency charge fees that are clearly stated?

Is the agency prepared to give you the best possible service? An agency cannot guarantee results on any specific date, but will often estimate an average recovery rate that one can expect.

Will the agency be sensitive to a consumer's individual situation? The agency should promptly notify you when it discovers a consumer who is a hardship case and recommend a proper procedure to follow.

CHAPTER THREE

STEPS TO MANAGE CREDIT SUCCESSFULLY

In my experience many businesses do not have credit management plants or any credit policies in place. Managing your business cash flow can be the single most important thing that can make or break your company, no matter if you are a new business or have been around for many years. There are some things you can do to make this credit management easier. The first thing is to manage your receivables, or hire someone to do it for you. Managing your receivable means you keep an eye on them, you stay on top of payments and run aging reports, and look at them! Another thing you need to do it make it as easy as possible for your customers to pay you, offer different types of payment options such as cash, credit or online payments. One of the most important things you can do to manage your business credit successfully is to have a credit policy in place with payment terms and that you can stick to. It doesn't help you to have a policy that you don't follow or that doesn't work for your business. You need to do the same with your collection procedures, make sure you have collection policies in place that are easy for you to carry out. You also don't want to forget accounts payable, keep your eye on your payables reports as well. The skills and resources you need in order to successfully manage your credit are:

Signed and filled out credit applications
Full knowledge of the FDCPA and any state or other Federal collection laws
Communication skills
Negotiation skills
Skip-tracing or location skills or resources
Mediation skills
Organizational skills

If you find these steps overwhelming or something you are not educated about and you don't want to dive right in, you may want to hire someone to be your credit manager, collections person or accounts receivable clerk to handle these aspects of your credit for you. If you decide to hire someone else to take on these tasks for you do some research and talk to other business owners who may have done this. You will want to have a clear understanding of what a bill and/or account collector does, for example, they collect payments by phone or by using letters to collect payments on past due invoices. They may negotiate repayment plans with customers and help them find a solution to get the bills paid off in full.

As of this writing there are no college degrees offered on being a bill collector, though there are classes you can take to educate yourself or an employee. My last book *The Guide to Getting Paid, weed out bad paying customers, collect on past due balances, and avoid bad debt*, as well as *The Ultimate Credit and Collections Handbook, the check IS in the mail* have been used in classrooms in colleges across the nation to educate business owners and credit professionals on the best practices for this job. As a bill collector a typical job description would include, finding your customers, through printing an aging report, who have overdue balances, and then trying to collect on those balances. They would also track down customers who may have an out of date address, disconnected phones or new jobs. They also need to have negotiation skills in order to negotiate payments when a customer is unable to pay the balance in full and needs to set up a repayment plan. In some instances this person would also be responsible for reviewing the terms of sale or payment with the customer if necessary. The most common way for a bill collector to contact someone that is past due is by phone and sometimes by mail. They must keep very specific records that include the dates and times of every conversation and the result of what action will be taken. The main job of your collector is to find a solution with the tools you provide that is acceptable to you and to your customer in order to get your bill paid in full as quickly as possible. Once your collector sets up a repayment plan with a customer it is their job to stay up to date and follow up with that customer to ensure those payments are made as agreed. They would also be responsible for taking action if those payments are not made. Being a collector is very stressful and keeping your collectors educated is vital to making this whole system work. To be a successful collector the person must be ready to face rejection, and speak to emotional people who can become angry. The collector must be able to have to stay polite and positive in a negative situation and be ready to offer solutions and help. I like to think of a bill collector as someone who is offering customer service to a customer that is in trouble. If you look at the job as a customer service rather than as a bill collector, it becomes a bit easier to remain calm, come up with solutions and help the upset customer calm down and agree to a beneficial solution that will help the bill get paid. Training and experience are the two keys to being successful as a bill collector, offer your collectors as much training as you can afford; it can't hurt and can only help you.

One of the most important things you must do in order to manage your credit successful is checking a customer's credit and deciding on a realistic credit limit based on their credit worthiness. Once you have a new customer walk in the door and they want to apply for a revolving credit account, you must check their credit history in order to make an educated decision on how much credit you want to extend to them or how much of a risk you are willing to take based on the credit limit you give them and their ability to pay you back. If you have a signed credit application you may pull a credit report or contact the references they provided. Take notes and always get the persons full name, title and extension that are providing you the reference information. Many people ask me what types of questions I should ask when checking references, so I want to give you a list of questions you can ask that can help you make an educated decision.

How long have you known this customer?
How long has this customer been doing business with you?
What payment method does this customer normally use?
Does the customer pay within terms, late or early?
What is this customer's average balance and how much of that is past due?
What is the average amount of this customer's normal order?
How often does this customer place orders with you?
What are this customer's payment terms with you?
Does this customer make many returns?
Does the customer take unauthorized discounts?
What has this customer's high credit been in the last year or 6 months?
Is the customer's account current right now, today?

When you contact a potential customer or customer's bank for a credit reference, many times you will have to fax over a copy of the signed credit application so they have proof that they have permission to share this information with you. Once you do this, there are specific questions you want to ask their bank.

What type of account do they have? Business, personal, savings, loan or checking?
When did they open this account?
What is their average daily balance?
Have they had any returned checks for any reason? If yes, when was the last one and how many in the last 6 months?
Do they have any outstanding loans? Are they current?
Are the loans unsecured or secured?
Are the loans being paid as agreed?

As you check someone's credit you want to keep an eye open for some red flags and just some general practices. For example, do they pay their other bills on time or late, are they frequently past due with other vendors, do they have a seasonal pattern when making payments, did they always pay on time but now pay late due to marital issues, the economy or unemployment, what are their anticipated monthly purchases, and will this customer agree to pay COD or cash on delivery while you check their credit worthiness.

Here are some specific steps that I have used when I handled credit applications. I thought that if I could outline my process it might help you come up with a process that works for your business.

New customer walks in the door. They are handed a "New Account Form" which can be your credit application. They sit down and fill it out or take it with them.

Office staff brings you the signed credit application to check so she can let the customer know if they are approved.

First thing to do is make sure the application is signed, and all the fields are filled out.

If you are a member of a credit bureau, and every place I worked as a credit manager was a member of at least one; you input the information into their website to get a copy of their credit report.

While you are waiting for the credit report, start calling the references listed on the credit application, paying special attention to the bank reference and what questions to ask. Most banks will ask you to email or fax a copy of the signed credit application to prove you have permission from the account holder to receive this information.

Once you have called each reference, and made notes you will know if this account is headed towards being a good or bad credit risk. Now take a look at the credit report.

On the credit report the person's name and addresses will be at the top, if they have a spouse or ex spouse, that information may also appear there. There will also be dates showing you how long that person lived at each address. Take a look at the different addresses, and how often this person moves. If there are many addresses and frequent moving around that could be a red flag. You don't want to sell something on credit to this customer only to have them move while they owe you money and not leave a forwarding address.

Next take a look at the employer information, their jobs will be listed with the most current first and the dates of employment for each. If someone jumps from job to job they could be a credit risk, so take a look at how often they change jobs and how long they stay at each one.

The header part of the credit report will give you a "summary" of this person's credit activity and history. It will tell you how much available money they believe is available after this person pays all of their bills, to pay you.

You can scan down to see the details of how much they pay to anyone who reports to this particular credit bureau. For example, the electric company may show each monthly payment and if it was on time or late. It will tell you how many payments were late and by how many days. It will tell you the amount of each payment and if they have any outstanding balance. The same will be true for the phone company, or a cell phone company, internet service, doctor bills, loans, credit cards, or anyone who reports to this credit bureau.

Be aware that some companies only report to one credit bureau. I have found that being a member of all three credit bureaus is beneficial because many times, one may have something the other does not list on their reports. For example, the electric company may report only to Experian and the phone company may only report to Trans Union.

When you look at this detail it will also tell you if the account has been closed and if it was closed by the creditor or the cardholder. If an account is closed by the cardholder you may want to ask them why or just note that this is a positive action. If the issuer closed the account it could be for non-payment but if the card holder closed the account, it could be just to improve their credit. If an account was placed with a collection agency, repossessed, sued in court or any actions taken for non-payment that will be listed there. If there was a bankruptcy that will be listed as well as if the person is deceased.

Based on calling to check references and looking at the credit application, you may be ready to make a decision on how much credit to approve this customer for. If you don't feel comfortable, now is the time to ask for more references and/or talk to the customer. Maybe they are disputing the very thing listed on their credit report – which could change everything.

Many people do not know how to decide on a credit limit for a customer. The way to do this is to take all the steps listed above so you have an idea on this person's credit worthiness. Take into consideration if they are a consumer or a business, and the orders they will place with you monthly. Most businesses offer 30 day terms, so you want to think of this in a monthly capacity. As an example, I worked at an oil company as a credit manager for years. When I was trying to extend credit to someone, after checking their credit I would take a look at the size propane or oil tank they had, how often they would need it filled and what the cost would be. Most times people had a 250 gallon tank, and back them the pre-buy price for oil was $.90 so a $250 credit limit would work for most of those people, if they had outstanding credit; maybe the limit was $500. For some people who had passable credit, but not outstanding credit, they might have a credit limit of $250 but could only have one outstanding invoice at a time, or they had to pay for their last delivery before they could receive another. As you try to set credit limits, just take a look at a customer's history or if they are a new customer, ask them how much they think they need to order each month, and if they don't have an idea, start low. You can always increase credit limits at a later time, based on payment and order history.

CHAPTER FOUR

TOP METHODS FOR IMPROVING COLLECTIONS

As we all know things have changed and keep changing, things we used to do before to improve collections are no longer effective, and so what can we do to improve our collections with the same or less effort? We have to change when things are changing and adapt to new market conditions and a new economy. We must change how we limit our credit risk, how we extend credit, how we get paid, and how we deal with customers who may fall onto hard times and need help paying their bills.

In the past we may have been able to overlook when a customer became just a little past due and eventually paid us, but now this may no longer be an option or it can be a red flag. Getting paid on time and in full begins with you; you need to "train" your customers to pay you on time and before anyone else. You need to make your bill be the most important bill that customer pays each month.

Some of the biggest changes have to happen within your company and credit department, so some of the things you can do to help your cash flow that you may have never done before include:

Assigning one person in your office to the larger accounts so they can build up a rapport with those customers is your best strategy. When customers have a "familiar" person or someone that they always deal with or know, they are more comfortable talking about the debt and coming to a payment resolution. Communication is important in keeping that relationship alive and healthy. In an article I recently read titled "What retailers should do if they cannot pay vendors within terms" they did a survey asking for suggestion on what retailers can do if they are having a difficult time paying their bills on time. An overwhelming 100% of the people surveyed agreed that they would be more patient and understanding if the retailer communicated with them honestly and worked with them to create a payment plan that they could stick to. Credit can be like marriage, with no communication it breaks down, so keep in touch, keep talking and asking questions and offer a reasonable solution to help your customers and yourself. Many people are private about their finances so having someone who can have a relationship with the customer or are familiar with the customer will help that customer communicate about financial issues more openly. They will feel more comfortable and will share more information.

Another way to improve your collections is to cancel any back orders until existing inventory is paid for. If this causes a big problem and you want to continue to fill orders for a customer that owes you money, offer to send future or backorders on a cash or COD basis with a couple or a few hundred dollars added on to the COD tickets to pay for the new order in full and get something towards the past due balance. The amount you add on to the COD ticket would depend on the amount the customer owes you, the amount they will be ordering and how much is realistically affordable to them. Maybe they could order a little less and pay COD for that order and still be able to pay a little on the past due balance. This way you create a win win situation, win for your customer because they still get the product from you that they need and win for you because you get paid for that order immediately and get a payment towards their past due balance.

Be careful opening new credit approved accounts. I recommend that you don't open a bunch of new accounts with large credit limits, or if you do, give the new account lower credit limits to start out with and let them prove to you based on their performance that they deserve a higher credit limit. You already know to get a signed credit application, but really analyze financial statements, bank statements and trade references. This will help you to weed out more credit risks and stop a problem before it starts.

Tenacity is one of your most important skills. It is up to you as the creditor to make sure your customers pay. Think of it as educating your customers on your payments terms, how you work, what you want and how they can do that. Even if you do everything right in the beginning, such as getting signed credit applications, limiting your risk, and calling customers that become past due, if you get lazy and don't follow up with these customers, they then see that you don't care and if you don't care, and they don't care, your invoice goes to the bottom of the payment pile. Now you don't have your most important payment tool which is communication. In my experience anyone who is paying you slowly is paying other slowly as well. The squeaky wheel get paid, when I was in debt I paid the people who called me and sent me letters first, in order to stop the calls and letters. I paid the others last. Keep that in mind when you decide to do nothing about your overdue accounts.

When someone becomes past due call them and take a credit card over the phone for the past due balance. If this happens realize that there may be a problem and re-evaluate their credit, make sure they are still worthy of the credit limit given to them and adjust it if necessary. Make sure to notify a customer if you change their credit limit. Some company may offer (or you can ask!) to have a credit card on file to charge any orders automatically as they become due. You can sell this to your customer as a way to have their invoices paid without having to think about it, without having to worry about becoming late, and without having to worry about you calling them or any late fees. If you offer an early pay discount, this can also be a way they can take advantage of that without any effort on their part, saving money themselves and helping you by getting the invoice paid and off the books. This system also helps a customer prevent having their credit limit lowered, their credit revoked, or having a late payment reported to the credit bureaus, affecting their credit score and hurting their business.

Another important tool that helps you get paid before your competition is being consistent. This goes along with following up on accounts. If you call once and never call again, everything you did prior to that phone call was for nothing. Being consistent lets your customers know you have not forgotten about them or the money they owe you. It lets them know that they are important to you as a customer and that you want to help them pay you so they can continue to be a customer. Remember, a bill collector is performing a customer service function and every customer likes to feel important. When you are consistent you show your customer you are on top of things, you are serious about your business, them as a customer, and about getting paid. Being consistent also means you have to have patience, be realistic, be nice and offer a solution or two. This goes a long way in getting paid from any customer. Most people that fall behind on payments never mean to fall behind, they really do want to pay you, but they are struggling themselves. If you can offer some understanding, offer some solutions, and be realistic, all of those things will help your customer to feel better about the situation, about doing business with you and they will do their best to pay you before another vendor who is calling them and maybe not being as nice or understanding.

Follow up quickly, follow up often and follow up consistently. More credit managers than I can count make collection calls and get a payment promise and think that is the end of it. This is never the case, once someone promises you any type of payment or sets up a payment arrangement, you need to send them a letter outlining that arrangement and confirming payments dates, payment amount and the new balance due. If you don't receive a scheduled payment, call them. When I was a credit manager and owned my collection agency, any time I set up any type of new payment arrangement with a customer, I would call them the day before they were to mail the payments to verify and confirm that the payment of a specific dollar amount would be mailed the next day. I would do this for the first 2-3 payments and then if they were on track, I didn't have to babysit the account so closely. I would say something similar to – "This is Michelle from ABC Company and I am calling to confirm that you will be mailing me a check for $100 tomorrow, Wednesday, July 29th towards your balance of $1000.00." When I would receive that payment, I would always send a confirmation letter thanking them for that payment and letting them know when the next payment is due and what their new balance was. You can use or see examples of these letters in my books of letters and forms, available on Amazon in paperback or for your Kindle, iPod, computer, phone or other electronic device.

This next tip is one I have done myself and had very good results with. I have told people who have attended my presentations to try this and the ones that have; have also had very good results. Send flowers. Send a bouquet in a basket with a card to a customer that is past due thanking them for being a customer and thanking them for their business. Only try this with a "newly" past due account, otherwise it isn't as effective. This shows the customer that you value them as a customer and want to continue doing business with them. Send the flowers from the company and then when the credit department calls about a bill they don't even have to let on that they know flowers were sent. Most times the customer will bring it up and thank you for the flowers and tell you they sent the check or are sending it today. I have found I don't even have to make another collection call; this really helps keep your bills at the top of the payables pile. This may not work for everyone, but when I find an unusual way to help you get paid, I want to share it with you.

If a customer is in a very dire situation and if you are able to, offer to suspend a payment or two or take payments twice a month rather than weekly. Getting paid twice a month is better than once a month or not at all. You can also offer discounts if the customer can pay the balance in full within a week or two, just be sure to have an expiration date on the offer. Another option is to lower the interest rate if you charge one or write off a late fee. These things could be just the incentive the customer needs to pay your bill. They may have to rob Peter to pay you, but it still gets your invoice paid. If the customer knows that you are willing to negotiate or work with them when they are having a hard time, they may take advantage of those options and pay your bills first.

Another method to improve your collections is to wait until your customer needs something from you. If your customer has an advertised sale or big event coming up that would be a good time to get any invoices paid. They will need to place orders to have stock for the sale or event and that is a good time for you to get them to pay any outstanding balances. Staying up to date on what your customers are doing can help you come up with creative ways to get paid, such as this one. Are your customers planning an expensive project, updating or remodelling? Are they having an open house or a sale, have their profits gone up or down, what are their current financial circumstances? All of this information can help you make a better decision and offers when you are talking about past due balances. Be flexible, statistics show that people are more willing to pay when a collector is willing to negotiate more affordable payments or offer another solution rather than making the unrealistic demand of payment in full before Friday.

If you don't already, start reporting good and bad debts to the credit bureaus. If your customers know that you report good and bad debt to the credit bureaus, they will pay you before someone who doesn't. Many businesses don't think to report good paying customers, so if you can offer this to your customers, they may always put your invoices at the top of the pile. Having you report any on time payments can only help their business and in this economy that is a huge perk that can drive payments to you.

Make sure your customers "understand" their balances, their pricing and discuss any discrepancies, such as shortage claims, mismatched PO#'s, discounts, and everything else to do with billing and payment and do this BEFORE the invoice is due. This can resolve any issues ahead of time to make sure you still get paid on time.

As you work on improving your collections ask yourself the following questions about your clients or customers in order to decide if you want to continue doing business with them. This can help you decide if they are too much work or hassle or if they are a good customer.

Do they have a pattern of paying other suppliers late and some on time? If yes, why?
Are they often past due with other bills? Which ones and why?
Have they run into financial problems causing them to pay later each month?
How long have they been in business and how have they been faring?
Who are their customers? Do they check their customer's credit before making a sale?
Do they have any competition? How does the competition look compared to them, are they doing better financially?
Do they have any collection accounts, liens, U.C.C. filings or judgments against them?

To improve your collections you need to really know your customers. I want to share with you some of the most common credit management errors and how to correct them. Being aware of the mistakes most commonly made can help you better manage your business credit by avoiding them.

Not checking a customer's credit history before extending a credit limit.
Not getting a signed and filled out credit application, agreement or contract before extending credit.
Not being familiar with Federal and/or state collection laws and unintentionally breaking one when dealing with a customer.
Overlooking small balances.
Not asking for your money because you hate asking for your money.
Not knowing when is the right time to turn the account over to a collection agency.
Not having any type of credit policy to follow and not following a credit policy.
Extending credit to anyone who walks in the door because "they seem like they will pay.
Not taking any action on returned checks.
Not using letters and forms to collect on past due balances.
Not having credit applications for your business.

Not checking credit.
Not understanding how to communicate with customers that pay on time.
Not using discounts and incentives to persuade customer to pay early.
Not knowing how to set up realistic payment schedules with customers.
Not knowing what to do if a customer files for bankruptcy.
Not training your collection staff.
Waiting too long to use a collection agency.
Not asking for your money because you don't want to make your past due customer mad.

If you have already made some of these mistakes there are things you can do to correct them. The first one should be to start enforcing your credit policy. Also, make sure your debtor is "worth" something before you sue them, if they don't have a job or bank account, or any asset there is nothing to attach or garnish if they do not pay. You have to decide how much time and money you want to spend chasing bad debt, especially when it is a small amount. Always ask for payment immediately when payment is due and research and sign on with a third party debt collection agency before you need one so when you do need them they are there and ready. Always check credit references, and remember if something doesn't seem right, it probably isn't. Ask for additional references or offer less credit until you feel comfortable that you can raise the limit based on the customer's ability to pay you. If you give a customer credit without checking their credit, they call the shots. Don't let that happen to your business.

In order to improve your collections you will need to do the following things:

Weed out your bad-paying customers.
Collect more of the money that is owed to you quickly and efficiently.
Use the most effective collection tactics.
Use a collection agency.
Measure your results.

The best advice I can offer you to collect more money quickly begins with not feeling guilty asking for your money. Develop credit policies or at least a list of payment rules everyone can follow. Keep on top of late payers, call them or send them a notice, but do something!

Above I mentioned payment rules, so I wanted to give you an example of what payment rules might be. This can be a one page list you type from your credit policy, and any and all of these things are interchangeable based on the order you will do things and what you will do.

Payment Rules (or the 1 page credit policy)

1. No sales will be made on credit without a signed filled out credit application being processed.
2. You must pay your bill within 28 days from the date on the bill.
3. If you become past due we will send you a friendly reminder letter.
4. If you still don't pay we will call you.
5. We will report the debt to the credit bureaus so it appears on your credit report.
6. At 90 days the account will be placed with a collection agency.
7. If you write us a bad check your credit is revoked and you will pay all fees cash only.

CHAPTER FIVE

GETTING PAID ON TIME: EXACTLY WHAT TO DO AND HOW TO DO IT

First, ask yourself, what do you do now when a customer becomes past due? Immediately make a list of things you want to happen when a customer becomes past due. Maybe you want to make a personal visit, or send a friendly reminder, or make a phone call. Decide what will work best for you and that you have the time to do and write it down. Write down 3 steps you can take when an account becomes past due, post it by your computer and start doing those things starting today whenever someone goes beyond their payment terms.

Next, make a list of things to do when a customer gives you an excuse as to why they can't pay their past due balance. This way when you get an excuse you won't be thrown off guard and will have a plan of steps to take in this situation. See chapter seven for excuses and what you can say in response.

If you are extending credit you need to protect yourself and your cash flow by limiting your credit risk. If you have any customers that are not paying you on time, they are destroying your cash flow and your ability to pay your own bills on time. Here is what to do and how to do it for your business.

Call every past due customer and ask for payment in full.
Start with the larger balance accounts and work your way down the list. Always begin every collection call asking for full payment and working your way down from there. In this economy it may not be feasible for someone to make the full payment so be prepared to offer payment plans or options. Try asking for half the balance now and the other half in two weeks. Remember to offer a solution to the customer to create a win-win situation for both of you.

Stop shipping orders to customers that owe you money.
If a customer is past due and they place a new order, put that order on hold or their account on hold until that balance is paid and you re-negotiate their payment terms for this new order. As soon as you put an order on hold pick up the phone to let the customer know and try to get payment over the phone.

Check every customer and potential customer's credit worthiness.
Because the economy has changed that means your customer's credit situations have changed. Folks who may have had great credit three or four years ago may not have such good credit now. Re-evaluate all customers credit limits to limit your risk and help keep your customers out of trouble.

Re-evaluate your payment terms.
Get paid sooner by changing your payment terms from net 30 or net 45 and by offering an incentive to customers to pay you early. Offer them an early pay discount, based on their sales. For example 2% 10, net 30, this way they will pay your bills first since they can save money. This helps your customer by saving them money and gets you paid faster.

Weed out the bad paying customers and fire some customers.
At least once a year or every six months you need to take a good look at your customer base and decide who the good and bad customers are so you can weed them out and get rid of them. Any customer that takes up your time or resources by not paying within your terms is not a good quality customer. If you have customers that do this often and are often past due or late think about firing them. You want a customer base that orders regularly and pays you on time, not customers who pay late, call to place more orders when they owe you money or waste your time explaining why they can't pay you. Once someone doesn't pay you on time, you start losing money.

In addition to the steps listed above you should try to implement these steps that can help you get paid on time. Just doing one new thing a week can make a big difference.

Make a phone call; this is the most effective way to get paid.
If the customer is local, make a personal visit.
Send a letter
Always call back if you get an answering machine.

Make sure every customer has a filled out and signed credit application on file with your company.
Set realistic credit limits for customers based on credit worthiness and order and payment history.
Put every customer with a past due balance on HOLD for new orders until those balances are paid.

Revoke the credit of anyone with a balance over 90 days and send them a letter letting them know. In my experience this provokes a phone call, re-opening the communication and discussion about payment.
Weed out your bad customers and fire them.

These things may all seem overwhelming, but break them down into smaller projects and they will go quickly and become habits. In order to be successful with the above steps there are some preventive steps you can implement immediately to make the above steps easier. Those steps are:

Stay on top of your receivables and what people owe, weekly if possible; remember it is just a customer service call. Contact a customer immediately if they become overdue, even just a little. Do not continue to ship products to a customer that is not paying on time. Send invoices immediately after products ship or service is performed.

You may be doing these tasks yourself or maybe you have a credit manager and a few collectors. In each case you need to make sure to train your credit department and collectors. Some of the things your collection department should be able to do include:

Identify the most common forms of credit activity
Name the three major credit reporting agencies and their functions.
Know Federal and state collection laws and their roles in relation to their job duties.
How to stay professional but be effective and firm.
How to open and close a collection call legally and professionally.
How to ask fact finding questions based on the reason for the past due balance.
Strategies and tools to motivate customers at different stages of past due balances.

Your collection department should be interested in people, and have good communication stills in person, on the phone and in writing. Collectors need to be persuasive and persistent, with the ability to deal fairly with people in often difficult situations. Be able to remain calm, negotiate, have office and computer skills and be able to explain and discuss financial matters clearly.

For over 20 years, I have been telling businesses that at least once a year they need to fire some customers. These would be the customers that don't pay you on time, take unauthorized discounts, order more and pay less. Anyone who gives you a hard time and talks to you about why they can't pay and when they can pay but why you need to ship them a new order is costing you money and wasting your time. This is how you weed out the bad customers. The good customers are the ones you should be talking to and spending time with, they pay you on time or early, they order frequently, don't take deductions or request proof of delivery, they don't waste your time and they also help make you money. You profit from these customers. The customers who don't pay and give you excuses are the bad kids in the room who are getting all of the attention when it should be the other way around.

The most effective way to collect any money that is owed to you is to make a personal visit to the person who owes the money. Most people do not do this, and so I offer you the second most effective way to get paid which is making a phone call and seems to be much less "scary" to people than making a personal visit.

If you are following your credit policy and run into customers that have not paid the first thing you should do if possible is visit them and ask them for the money. If that is too much for you, start buying your morning coffee where they get theirs, and say good morning. Then go back to your office and call them, then call them again. This works for consumer debt or business debt, I have done this successfully with both types. If they don't respond, keep calling them, send a collection letter, and put their account on hold. Keep buying coffee where they buy coffee in the morning, or the newspaper, or lunch, and say hello. They know that they owe you money; you don't need to say anything about it. It has been my experience that they eventually will approach you and bring it up, re-opening the communication or they will just start getting their coffee/newspaper/lunch somewhere else.

Report the debt to the credit bureaus, and revoke their credit, send them a final notice letting them know this has been reported and that their credit has been revoked, send the letter in a flat rate priority mail envelope. If they still ignore you, take them to court and move on.

This all may seem very drastic and severe but it is not. If you don't do these things you probably won't get paid anything. Some of the most common and least effective things businesses do with past due accounts are:

Ignoring the account and hope they will pay.
You don't call because they don't want to make the past due customer mad.
You don't have any recourse because they never got a signed credit application.
You don't have specific payment terms on any of their paperwork.
You never call or mail the customer, no monthly statements are sent.
You accept debtor's excuses, do nothing and don't get paid.

At a certain point it starts to cost you money to try and collect on an account, when that happens you might consider using a third party collection agency to work those accounts for you. You should use a collection agency if your customers are ignoring your calls and letters or if their mail is being returned for any reason and the phone is disconnected. When you hire a collection agency look for an agency that specializes in your industry. For example, if you work at a hospital look for a medical collection agency. Look for an agency that is licensed and bonded, and a member of any organizations. Ask for existing and past customers and call them, ask how they like the agency or why they don't use them anymore.

When you start thinking about hiring a collection agency, you are probably like every other business owner out there wondering what to look for and how to choose the best agency. When you look up collection agencies online or in your local phone book there are some things you should look for. You want to try and find a collection agency that is familiar with your specific business. If you are a medical office, an agency that collects on student debts won't do you much good. An agency that is familiar with your type of customers and debt will know better questions to ask and solutions to offer based on that industry. For example, I was a credit manager for an oil company, doing collections for an oil company, the questions I might ask a past due customer would differ from the questions you would need to ask when collecting on past due credit card debt or an auto loan. Ask other people in your industry who they use for a collection agency to get an idea of what your options are.

Choose an agency based on your customers, are your customers consumers or other businesses – most collection agencies specialize in either consumer or commercial debt collections.

Does the agency belong to any trade associations, a local chamber of commerce or rotary club? Being a member of a networking group or the Better Business Bureau gives an agency some credibility and you can call those groups for a reference on the agency. Also check the Better Business Bureau website for a history and to see if there are any complaints against the agency, what they were or are and how long ago. If you find negative information about an agency, you could talk to them or do more research but it may be better to find an agency with no complaints against them.

With all the horror stories out there about abusive debt collectors, you want to make sure the agency you hire isn't one of them. Ask the agency about the process they use to collect a debt; will they be sensitive to an individual situation? The agency should quickly notify you if they discover a consumer who may be a hardship case and recommend a procedure to follow to help that debtor. In the new economy we are dealing with, this happens more now than it has in the last few years so it is important to be aware of it and know what you will do if it happens.

Third party collectors must comply with Federal and state laws where they are located and where the consumer that owes the money is located. By checking references you will be able to determine if the agency you are interested in has a history of breaking these laws and being sued for violations. If you find an agency like that, run away!

As you look for a collection agency to use for your business, you may find some websites offering debt collection services that you aren't too sure about. Some of the things to keep an eye out for when you are looking for an agency are to make sure they have a physical address on their website, and not just a PO Box. Look for a phone number, email and contact information to be easily available. Look for an agency that has an "About Us" page and gives you a little history about their agency and the people who work there. If there is a photo of the owner or any employees with contact emails, that is a good sign. I see so many collection agency websites that don't look professional, the links don't work, they don't list their address or have photos of anyone who works there or may own the agency, and no contact us option. That is a website I would be leery about.

See if they have any logo's to any trade associations or memberships they may have that you can contact to see if they are a member and ask how long they have been a member. Also ask if there have ever been any complaints about them.

Make sure their rates or pricing are readily available on their website, and look for testimonials from happy customers. Ask questions, now is the time to ask.

Look out for agencies that don't have a physical address or a phone number listed on their website and that also don't list that they belong to any trade associations or local networking groups. If you don't get a live person when you call, and get a recording instead – you might want to consider that when your customers may call to make payments they will get that same recording. Don't you hate it when you call somewhere and you don't get a live person? Make sure the agency you choose represents how you would like your customers to be treated and remember that the agency you choose is a reflection of you and your business. Make sure the agency is licensed and bonded in the states you will hire it to collect in and ask them if they have errors and omissions insurance. If an agency has the lowest price out there, make sure to do your research. Cheaper is not always better and you do get what you pay for. No matter which agency you decide to go with get a signed contract and make sure you have a copy. Know what the agency will do for you and what your responsibilities are.

As you research collection agencies and take all of this information I have given you into consideration, here is a short list of the questions to ask when making a decision to hire a collection agency:

- Do they specialize in a specific type of debt collection – consumer/commercial, medical, retail, utilities, etc?
- What associations or networking groups do they belong to? Are they in good standing?

- What are their collection procedures do they only send letters or do they send letters and make phone calls, how often do they call, and can you see copies of the letters they send out?
- Have they had any or excessive complaints against them for law violations? How often, how many, when was the last time, how were they resolved?
- Do they list all contact information clearly on their website, correspondence and do they identify themselves when they answer the phone? Do you get a live person or a recording when you call? What will the debtors get when they call?
- What is the pricing structure, is it a flat monthly fee or a commission? What is the commission? Is that across the board or do I get a discount based on the volume of accounts I place with your agency? Do you disperse payments monthly? Do you send out update reports on accounts and if so, how often?
- Ask for the names and phone numbers of current customers, call them. Ask them:
    - How long have you been using this agency?
    - How has their service been so far?
    - How many accounts do you normally place with them a month?
    - What do you like the most about this agency?
    - What do dislike about them?

Now that you have decided on a collection agency to use for your company, you have to figure out when is it time to use a collection agency. This is different for every business out there. Depending on your terms, you might place accounts for collection after 90 days or after 120 days. Some businesses place accounts with a collection agency at 65 days. If you are going to do some in house collections before sending accounts over to an agency, you may end up sending accounts sooner than later. This is because as you work on the accounts you will become familiar with the signs to look out for that indicates when someone may be running into financial trouble and you want to make every effort to get paid. As an account ages, the chances of collecting on that account decrease dramatically, so the sooner you place accounts, the better. It sometimes becomes a better use of your company's time and resources to concentrate on other aspects of your business.

When an account reaches 90 to 120 days past due, it's time to consider placing them with your collection agency. Some people place accounts at 60 days, some wait well over a year. Just remember that the sooner you place an account with a collection agency the better your chances are of getting paid. This is why some agencies will charge a higher commission on old accounts. They are very hard to collect, so keep that in mind when you decide when you want to place your accounts for collection.

I just mentioned the signs to look out for that indicate when someone may be running into financial trouble and you want to make every effort to get paid. These are the signs to look for that you may need to place an account with a collection agency:

- A fairly new (less than a year) customer does not respond to invoices, statements or letters. For some unknown reason the customer will not or cannot pay. You can keep your losses down by placing an account like this for collection sooner than later.
- Your payment terms fail. In some cases irresponsible customers pay when and if they want to. This group is responsible for 25-50% of the cost of collections. Determine the customers who may play payment games with you and get rid of them.
- The customer is making repetitious, unfounded complaints. Make sure you have the documentation to support the debt and place them for collection. Spend your time with customers that order consistently, pay on time and deserve your attention.
- The customer starts denying responsibility for the debt. Without professional collection help, these accounts are time consuming to you and your business.
- The customer has marital difficulties. It has been my experience personally and professionally that delinquency goes along with marital problems. In this situation your best bet is to quickly place the account with an agency before the problems get worse or the disappearance of one or both of the responsible parties. People start getting separated and moving, mail starts getting returned and phone numbers change. Let an agency locate the customers and do the collection work for you to resolve the debt as quickly as possible.
- Starting a pattern of paying late, it may start slowly and then the balances owed will become later and larger.
- Frequent address and/or phone number changes.
- Frequent changes in their job, where and when they work, how much they make.

A collection agency is a service business that helps businesses collect on accounts that are delinquent. Collectors have a vast knowledge of collection techniques, technology and compliance issues. Using a collection agency will save you time and give you better results than you might get on your own.

Collection agencies spend all day every day collecting debt. Some collectors are on the phone all day calling debtors about bills owed to their clients, trying to work with them to get the bill paid, sometimes setting up payment arrangements, or sending verification of a debt that someone is disputing.

Collection agencies also do skip tracing, this is the process of locating a debtor that has had their mail returned, maybe the phone is disconnected and they don't work at the last known job you had on file. The agency now has to locate them in order to even begin trying to collect for you. This service is normally included in the commission fee you pay the agency.

Most collection agencies also report the debts to the credit bureaus UNLESS the creditor has already reported the debt. If you report debts to the credit bureaus, make sure to let your agency know so that they don't also report it. Having the debt reported by the agency is also normally included as a service you pay for through the agencies commission rate.

Once you decide on a collection agency, they may provide you with online or printed forms to list your accounts on. In some cases you may be able to upload spreadsheets of accounts directly to them or to their collection software. Give as much information as possible because having accurate information about the account will improve collections. In all cases, the minimum information should include:

- The correct, full name, address and any phone numbers and email addresses of the customer
- Name of the customers spouse, if they have one
- Let them know if the mail has been returned and for what reason
- Customer and spouse's occupation or last known job and phone number
- Names of relatives, friends, neighbors and references (normally found on the credit application)
- Summary of any disputes or problems

- Date of last transaction, order or payment
- Nicknames, aliases or a maiden name if you know it

If you have had all of your customers fill out a credit application, most or all of the above information can be found on there. The summary of disputes or problems should be documented in your computer and can just be printed out or emailed with the accounts.

Cooperate with your collection agency, rely on their experience, diligence and judgment for the best and quickest results and promptly refer any contact from the customer back to the collection agency.

Don't place your accounts with more than one agency. Make sure that if you decide to change agencies that the accounts are only being worked on by one agency. Collection agencies fees are based on results, not on the time spent on the account. Don't expect payments to be made immediately.

When I owned my collection agency, I would have some clients who would place 1-3 accounts per year and would fax over a delinquent account to collect at 3:00 and then call the next morning to ask me if I collected the money. If you do things like that, no agency will want to work with you. Once an agency processes an account you place with them, they have to input it into their computer and get the initial collection letter in the mail. They can't do anything until the debtor receives that letter and even then have to give the debtor 30 days by law to request verification or dispute the debt. So, don't call your agency the day after or the week after you place accounts with them for an update.

Expect your collection agency to send you a monthly statement showing which accounts paid, what date they paid, how much they paid, how much of that goes to the collection agency and how much you will receive. Many agencies are now offering a secure website where you can sign in and look at your accounts and see up to date information on the collection action taken and if any payments have been made. Some agencies will also send updates on accounts at other times or if requested. Talk to your agency to see what they can offer you.

Once you start using a collection agency you will be excited to have taken care of all the bad debt floating around your receivables and anxious to see results. Having been a credit manager using collection agencies and having been an agency owner I want to tell you what not to do so that you can have a successful working relationship with your collection agency.

Don't call weekly for updates, ask if they can send updates or if they have an online option or another way you can satisfy this need for weekly updates. When you call collection agencies to ask for updates, they are spending the time they would be trying to collect your money, talking to you. Let them do their job.

Don't negotiate a payment with your customer after placing an account with a collection agency and if you do that – don't withhold the fact that the debt has been paid from the collection agency. Not only is it illegal for them to continue trying to collect on a debt that has been paid, it violates your agreement. Let your agency know if someone pays you directly so they can report the debt as paid to the credit bureaus and close it off their books, they will charge you the commission on your next statement.
I said this before but don't place your accounts with more than one agency. No one wins in that situation.

Most collection agencies charge a commission or percentage based on the many factors of the accounts they are trying to collect. Some agencies charge a flat monthly fee and some charge per letter or call.

If an agency charges a commission, it will normally be a percentage for "standard" accounts. That would be any accounts that are maybe 60 days old, have a good address and phone number and the debt is pretty collectible. When I had my agency, my basic collection rate was 25%. If an account was under $75 or over 1 year old my commission rate was 50%. When I had a large client placing many accounts weekly or monthly, I would give them a special rate based on the number of accounts they would place and how often as well as the age of the accounts and the dollar amounts. Second placements were always at a 50% commission rate. This would be accounts they had placed with another collection agency in the past that was unable to collect for them.

Some agencies will charge a flat monthly fee based on the number of accounts you place, how frequently you place them, the dollar amounts, and age. They may also charge per letter or per phone call and let you decide the frequency of each. Collection agencies may also offer other paid service, check out their websites and compare to see what the average free structure is and what works for you.

Most collection agencies send payments out monthly and some may offer this service twice a month. Quite a few agencies even offer online updates on the payments and the status of your accounts that they are working on. You no longer have to wait a month to find out who paid, you can search online or even call for an update.

Remember that when you place accounts with a collection agency, that doesn't guarantee that the debt will be paid and the agency certainly never guarantees a time frame for it to be paid. This is why the commission pay structure works well.

Many businesses that use collection agencies write the balances off to bad debt when they place them with a collection agency. If you do this, any money the collection agency collects for you is gravy. It is money you were not expecting to receive. With this in mind give your agency some time to process and work on the account. Agencies also have to give the debtor 30 days to request verification of the debt and/or dispute the debt by law.

Once you decide to turn your past due accounts over to a collection agency, be prepared for those customers that wouldn't return your calls, to call you. This doesn't always happen but it is very common. It has been my experience that the customer will call the business once they receive notification from the collection agency that they are handling the account. When this happens just remember to refer the customer back to the collection agency and let the agency know what contact has been made so they can follow up. I have also found that many customers will just mail the original creditor a check once they receive a letter from the collection agency. If this happens, let the agency know right away. The agency can take care of the account, close it out and charge you their commission on their next statement.

This sometimes makes a business feel uncomfortable, especially if it is a small business, so I always tell them to say it is out of their hands, that their book keeper or accountant handles that and it is a policy they have to follow. This pushes off the blame but hopefully you still get paid.

Sometimes a customer will come back to you for services or products after they have paid off a collection agency. Do not extend credit to this customer if you decide work with them at all. Once you have placed an account with a collection agency to get paid, only accept cash payments, up front. This customer cost you money when they didn't pay their bill, if they continue to purchase from you and have to pay cash, you might recoup your losses.

I want to give you more specific things you can do to get paid on time. Some of those things start even before the first order is placed. One of those things is don't assume that your customers know your credit policy. Many businesses have their credit policy printed on the back side of their credit applications so that the customer gets a copy. When I worked as a credit manager we added our credit policy, terms and conditions to our monthly statements, the back of the credit applications and it was a handout the sales department gave to new customers when they gave them a credit application to fill out, we would also give them one in the office if someone came in to fill out a credit application. We hung a copy in a frame in the waiting room and front office and the payment terms and conditions were on every email we sent out.

This may seem like a broken record but keep your customers credit records current. Otherwise they are useless to you and don't help you limit your credit risk. This is one of the biggest mistakes creditors make; they get a credit application in 2010 and never re-evaluate that customer again. Things change; including our customers credit, make sure you are protected.

Keep the lines of communication open, make your first call about a past due balance a customer service call. Call to make sure they received the invoice, that they received the products with no problems or satisfactory service and thank them for being a customer. I have done this successfully for many business to business invoices.

Try to correct or resolve any discrepancies before the invoice is due. This could include any shortages or pricing errors, but whatever the problem is, identify it before the due date so you can still get paid on time.

Some other ways to help you get paid faster include:

Offering early payment or term payment discounts
Start charging penalties for late payers.
Get payment up front.
Assign one collector to specific accounts regularly.
Cancel any back orders until existing inventory is paid for.

Be cautious when extending credit to new customers.
Call for a credit card payment immediately on a past due balance.
Be consistent.
Have patience, be realistic, be nice and offer a solution.
Follow up.
Thank the customer.
Report good and bad debt.
Always follow your collection policies.
Change your collection letters frequently.
Follow up immediately on a "short" payment or an un-agreed upon partial payment.
Have one person in charge of "large" accounts.
Speak to a manager or owner when making calls, go right for the decision maker.
Update your records often and make sure you have current phone numbers and addresses.
Make sure your invoices have the due date clearly noticeable.
Act immediately when an account gets a few days overdue.
When setting up payment arrangements remember that you want as much as you can get as frequently as you can get it.
Reduce minimum orders; you could possibly get more orders for less money paid up front.
Send demand letters in priority mail envelopes; it is more effective than certified mail.

When you use collection letters as a tool to get paid you have to remember that many collection letters go right into the trash can. Having been a bill collector and a debtor I know how many envelopes are thrown away unopened. You carefully word your letter, check it over and over, make changes and then it never sees the light of day. Your envelope has to be different in a way that gets it opened. The envelope is the first impression; it needs to scream, "OPEN ME!" An invoice or a bill doesn't do that. Some things that have worked for me include using enveloped that are different shapes, colours and sizes. Designing your envelope for "eye flow", studied show that people will look at their name, any comments below that return address and then the postage. Make sure the customer's name and address are correct, many times that is a key reason an envelope isn't opened and just thrown away. I have seen this happen at the post office, someone receives a bill or collection letter that is a form letter and says, they can't even spell my name right, they don't know me, and it goes in the trash unopened. Stamp or print something on the outside of the envelope in a bold print or colour, something such as confidential or important.

CHAPTER SIX

TELEPHONE COLLECTIONS BEST PRACTICES

Collecting money is a job most people don't want or shy away from. When you are the one making collection calls you need to remind yourself that the person you are calling can be embarrassed, stressed, angry or defensive. With this in mind it is important to have a plan in place before you begin calling people. Some things to think about before you pick up the phone are what type of solution can you offer, and what payment options are available, also remain calm and be professional no matter the response you get.

It is important to communicate confidence when you are speaking to anyone on the phone but especially a past due customer. You have to be able to stay in control of the call and the only way to do that is to be confident and prepared. When you start making collection calls you want to already know what the laws are that you must follow, these laws vary depending on the type of collector you are and where you are collecting. Another thing to keep in mind is that everything you do represent your company or the company you work for. How you talk, collect money, send out invoices, and handle tough situations. Remember that one way to appear more confident when you make collection calls include your first impression, so be confident. Come up with a greeting that says you are happy, pleasant and confident. When your customer answers the phone and realizes you are calling about a past due invoice, they will not be happy. You must portray confidence and not a dull boring message. Smile when you talk on the phone, it will be noticeable in your voice. Your voice should be loud enough to be heard clearly, not to loud but not too soft. You want your customer to hear you and understand what you are saying. Sit up straight in your chair and imagine the debtor is sitting across from you. Even when you are on the phone, maintain "eye contact" by staying focused on the call. Don't get distracted by others in the office or email. Relax and sit up straight, don't fidget with your pen or computer. Use your face, voice and posture to send your confidence over the phone lines.

Before you pick up the phone you will want to take a look at a customer's file. Any time you speak to a customer, make notes on the computer with the date and time and never call a customer without having their history in front of you. Once you place the call, if you are calling a business, ask for the person who placed the order, or the owner of the business or an authorized book keeper. If the debt is a consumer debt only speak to the person who legally owes you the money. Never discuss any overdue accounts with an unauthorized person, such as a receptionist, neighbour, friend, relative or co-worker. Once you have the owner or customer on the phone identify yourself and your business and state why you are calling. If the customer tells you they cannot pay anything, listen to them and then explain that you understand that they cannot pay in full right now but that you do need a payment. Start at 80% of the total past due balance and go down from there. At the end of the call, repeat the payment schedule to the customer and make a note in the customer's account. Whenever you make a payment arrangement like this, you will need to send a follow up letter the same day confirming the arrangement, due dates, amounts and new balance due. Include a payment envelope to speed up the payment.

Collectors can be their own worst enemies when making collection calls. As a consultant, I work with business professionals who want to engage their listeners, whether they are addressing employees, customers or colleagues. Never pick up the phone to call a past due account without researching the account history before the call. Review a customer's account before calling to ask for the money. It is your job to be prepared for any excuse or question the customer asks. If you are not prepared for everything, you will falter, lose your confidence and lose control of the call.

I know you are on the phone and the customer cannot see you but staying focused is important. You must practice eye contact when on the phone; imagine the customer is sitting across from you. This focus will carry through the phone lines in your voice. A customer can tell if you are distracted or not paying attention, which tells them you don't really care. Speak simply and clearly and be brief and to the point. You have other calls to make.

Dress the part. Dressing the part will help you feel more confident, efficient and professional, all the things you want to come across in your voice on the call. Great communicators always rehearse important presentations. Most bad presentations are the result of failing to practice talking out loud. Making debt collection calls is the same thing. You need to practice to be successful and stay in control of the call. The only way to be ready for every excuse is to make calls or practice with other collectors. You can practice into your answering machine to record your voice and see how you sound.

Don't be boring and dull, grab the attention of the customer when you call, tell them who you are and why you are calling. Then give them some details and tell them what action you want them to take – pay now over the phone, mail a check etc. Don't call a past due customer without a plan in mind of what you want them to do. This is your call to action. If you don't tell the customer specifically what you want them to do and when you want them to do it and then don't follow up on that action, don't expect it to happen.

When you make collection calls, the way to be successful is to be clear, keep it simple and remember that your goal is to get paid something. One of the most important things you can do to be a successful bill collector is to listen. Listen to the customer so you can help them pay you. Consider what they tell you, try to understand and come up with a solution that fits that scenario.

Reviewing an account before contact is crucial to your success. Know what you want to talk about before you call, know what solutions you can offer for payment, know if there were any discrepancies or shortage and be able to discuss and resolve them. Be reasonable; treat people with dignity and respect. Being professional and helpful when you are trying to do a difficult job such as collecting money is a necessity.

Be very clear – you cannot be clear enough – when you are talking about finances or it can get confusing. Be as concise as you can. Good business communicators use simple language to discuss complex issues. Keep a positive attitude, making collection calls will never be fun, but if you are going to be doing it, be positive, and have patience. Your job is to get the person on the other end of the phone to feel like paying off a debt and you are going to help them do that. Be nice; thank them when they make a payment promise or a payment over the phone. A little courtesy in this job goes a long way.

To recap, here are my top 12 ways to collect more money over the phone:

1. Be confident.
2. Be prepared.
3. Express urgency to the customer.
4. Smile
5. Listen.
6. Sit up straight.
7. Stop fidgeting and squirming.
8. Focus.
9. Dress professionally.
10. Know the call to action you want from the customer.
11. Be ethical, courteous and polite.
12. Take notes and follow up quickly, follow up often and consistently.

Each customer's situation is different. You may have to call someone who has been a customer for 25 years and now they may have filed bankruptcy or their spouse is deceased. Maybe you are calling a new customer that has only been a customer for 3 months but is now past due and you don't know the reason but you see they are ignoring your calls and letters.

You need to research each situation before you begin, this will give you the information and tools you need to identify what kind of debtor you are working with and what action needs to be taken. Look at your customer's history for more information. Being informed is the best collection tool you have. When I was a collector I would read the obituaries every day. I was a credit manager at a local oil company and had many local customers. Many times a debtor would have told me about a spouse in the hospital or I would recognize a name of someone I had been calling, so I could note the death on their account and take appropriate action. You want to avoid calling a deceased customer or their family right away, give them time to deal with their loss before calling again but make a note on the account.

As you train your phone collectors or start learning yourself some of the things you will need training on include developing your telephone voice and redefining your listening skills. For example, when you call a past due customer and tell them who you are and why you are calling, wait for them to reply. No matter how long the pause is, let them break the silence. Many collectors have a hard time doing this, the silence can be uncomfortable, but it is important that you let the customer break the silence with some type of reply/information so that you can help them pay you by understanding their situation.

You will also need to be prepared to manage the emotional side of the call. Debtors or past due customers will get upset that you are calling them, even though they know they owe you money and it is past due, this is something that normally happens with each call. Some will cry, yell at you, swear at you and hang up on you. When someone starts telling you their "life story" and how and why they cannot possibly pay you, you need to be able to first listen and then offer a solution to get the debt paid, such as a payment plan or maybe a different option for payment.

It is always a good idea to have a pre-call plan. Before you dial make sure you know the invoice number, date of the invoice or shipment, the total amount due, how much of that is past due, the payment history, details of the past due order and if there were or are any disputed items. When the debtor asks you any question you want to be able to answer immediately, this shows the customer or debtor that you are serious.

Before your call prepare what you are going to say or your opening statement. Your opening statement should be brief and to the point. You need to identify yourself and your company, and then state why you are calling and what you want. An example:

Collector: Hi this is Michelle from KTM Auto calling about your balance of $500.00 on invoice #123 dated 4/1/2012. I am calling today to take your payment over the phone to clear this past due balance from your account. Would you like to pay with a debit or credit card or a check over the phone today?

STOP! Let the customer answer your question and remember to always assume the debtor will pay. By asking questions with precision and making the transition over to the payment arrangement in your opening remark you have been very clear as to who you are, why you are calling and what you want the customer to do.

Example of how the call "could" go:

> Debtor: I can't pay, I don't have any money.
> Collector: Are you or your spouse working?
> Debtor: Yes, but I just started a job and don't get paid for two weeks.
> Collector: What day do you get paid?
> Debtor: Fridays.

Collector: Okay, how about if you mail a money order or check for $25 on Saturday from your first pay check and then I will call you next week to set up a regular weekly affordable payment for you?

Notice in the example I did not ask the debtor if they could pay $25 – never ask a debtor what they can pay, they will always give you the lowest amount. You need to take into consideration the circumstances, how past due they are, and the balance due. Then offer a realistic option so you don't scare the debtor away, you want them to be able to pay you and you want to keep the lines of communication open. If you scare them away in the beginning they will not pick up the phone when you call next time.

Remember to be positive and get a payment agreement. Once you have repeated what is happening with their account and payment send them a confirmation letter with a payment envelope. Copies of the confirmation letter and every other letter you will need can be found in my books of letters and forms available on Amazon and MichelleDunn.com. Once you send the confirmation letter call them on the Friday before the payment is to be mailed to remind them about making that payment. An example:

Collector: Hi This is Michelle from KTM Auto, calling to confirm you will be mailing a money order to me at (state company name/address) for $25 tomorrow, Saturday.

As you make these calls remember that you must do the following to be successful:

Manage the emotional side
Prepare your pre-call plan
Make the opening statement
Ask questions with precision
Make the transition to the payment arrangement
Handle objections
Close the call

An example of closing the call could be:

Collector: Okay, on Saturday (insert date), you will mail me a money order for $25 in the envelope I sent you last week after we spoke. Then you will send me $25 a week, every Saturday until May 15th.

CHAPTER SEVEN

TELEPHONE COLLECTION SCRIPTS AND EXCUSES

One of the questions I am most often asked in this industry is for effective scripts collectors can use to make actual collection calls and for information and examples of how to deal with different customer excuses. In this chapter I want to give you some scripts you can use or customize to use within your business and industry and also some of the most common excuses and how you can respond in a positive way that will help you to get paid.

We talked a bit about your pre-call plan in the last chapter so I want to give you some steps you can take to help you come up with your pre-call plan. Picture yourself getting ready to make a collection call, you need to get your opening remarks ready, to do this you have looked up the customer's account, have all the important information in front of you and you pick up the phone and dial. Your opening should be to:

1. Identify the customer; make sure you have the right person on the phone.
2. Identify yourself by first and last name and the name of your company.
3. Always start off asking for payment in full.
4. STOP and LISTEN.

Once the customer answers you, you will move on to the next part of your call, the body of the call. The body of your call is:

1. Determining your approach, is this the first call, if not - how did they respond last time?
2. Overcome any objections or excuses they give you.
3. Establish the payment date.
4. Get an agreement from the customer.

Once you have done those things you will move on to closing the call. To close the call you want to summarize what you agreed upon in the call, reiterate to the customer the amount of the payment, when it will be dropped off or mailed, and what will happen if the payment is not received as agreed by a certain date.

The next part of the call doesn't happen until right before the payment is due. This is the follow up portion of the call. Always send a confirmation letter on the day of the call and call back immediately if payment is not made. Do not wait.

Here is a list of things you should do as an example of following up on a collection call and payment promise.

1. When they tell you on Wednesday, that they are sending the check Friday, hang up the phone and mail a confirmation letter stating this.
2. Call them on Tuesday to verify the check will be mailed tomorrow.
3. Call them on Friday to verify the check was actually mailed.
4. Call them on Tuesday when you don't have the check.

The Squeaky Wheel gets the grease or in this case, gets paid!

I want to share some excuses and objections that customers might say to you as you make collection calls. If you can be prepared for any excuse or objection you will be much more effective. You need to have a response ready for any excuse so that you can reach your goal of getting paid from this customer. Many of the excuses on this list are actual excuses I have been told over the years making collection calls, others have been told to me by others who work in the field. I started out with some business to business excuses and then consumer debt excuses.

We didn't budget your bill for this year
The invoice has to be approved by another department
We are waiting for our customers to pay us so we can pay you
We did not order this
We did not receive the order
The check is on (somebody's) desk waiting to be signed, and they are on vacation
The book keeper is sick or on vacation
The computer is down
Your invoice is not on my list

I don't have your invoice
Accounts Payable only takes calls on Tuesdays between 1 and 3
The check is ready to mail it just hasn't been signed yet
I fired my contractor so I don't have a building to work out of
I brought you a check and your office staff wouldn't take it because something didn't match
Our company checks were stolen during a robbery so I am waiting for new checks from the bank
I am operating at a loss
My biggest customer just filed bankruptcy
We just changed banks and don't have checks yet
We are too busy to pay our bills right now
We are growing faster than we planned and don't have enough capital
We are having cash flow problems right now

Some consumer debt excuses:

The check is in the mail
I already paid that or I thought I already paid that
I don't have any money
I'm divorced and my ex-husband/wife is supposed to pay that bill
I didn't receive all the items I ordered
There was a problem with the order
I suddenly got sick and have medical bills to pay so I can't pay you
I lost my job
My wife/husband handles the bills
I'll try
You are harassing me
I'll pay in full when I get my Christmas club money, tax return, win the lottery
Hold on a minute – then they hang up
I can't get a loan or borrow the money to pay you
My insurance company should have paid that
When I have some extra money, I'll pay you
I have more important bills to pay
I'm filing for bankruptcy
I lost my glasses and can't read my bills or the letters you sent me
My car is broken down and the nearest mailbox is 10 miles away
That person is deceased, and when you call back a week later that person is not home right now
I didn't know I had to pay that

I was robbed of my mail at the post office while trying to mail your check
I can't find my check book but when I do, I will send you a check
I am waiting for it to stop raining
I'm sick, I can't pay anything
I was in a bad car accident and lost my memory
Our dog chewed up all our checks
I hurt my leg playing ball and can't get to the phone, post office, bank
I don't pick up the call when I hear your voice on my machine
I didn't receive the order (even though POD's prove it was delivered)
I didn't receive the invoice (even though it has been sent multiple times)

Now that you have these excuses in the back of your mind, I want to talk about the collection call. There are many parts to a collection call. It begins with your pre-planning of the call, your opening statement, then actually making the call and the body of the call dealing with excuses and objections and then closing the call.

The pre-planning of your call is when you review the customer's account and history as well as their payment history. You will think about re-payment plans you can offer this customer or solutions to any excuse or objections so that when you are on the call you have a couple of different options. Before you dial you will make sure you know who the right person is to talk to and ask for that specific person. This could be the person who signed the credit application or contract or the person who placed the order or the owner of the company.

Now that you have pre-planned your call you dial. Once the phone is answered get the correct person on the phone, you don't want to start talking about a debt with the wrong person. If you are doing business to business collections ask for accounts payable or the book keeper. Identify yourself (first and last name) and your company or the company you are calling for or representing. State why you are calling and ask them if they have processed your invoice #123 for payment. Listen to any objections or excuses and then answer those excuses. Once you have answered the objection, to stay on track say something such as, "John, I have to report back to my supervisor today on your balance, please let's agree on something I can tell him/her regarding your account. Can you send a partial payment of $(give specific amount based on the balance) today?" Depending on what this customer owes you, start asking for payment in full and then go down to 80% of the total bill and go down from there. Confirm the payment agreement details on the phone and send a confirmation letter.

As a customer gives you excuses or objections on the phone, you will learn to recognize these signs. When someone is giving you excuses or objecting in any way that is the time to take action, don't wait. If you don't know how to respond to a specific objection or excuse, check your company credit policy and talk to your manager. Update that particular customer's credit file, check their contracts and credit applications and make sure they are up to date and still credit worthy for the amount of credit you have extended to them. Especially check back with their bank to see if they might be having financial trouble so you can take steps to limit your credit risk and protect yourself and your business. Another very important step is to visit the customer if possible, and if it is not possible, review their account and give them a call to talk to them as if you were personally visiting them. This extra attention will help you limit your risk. The key here is to do something and not to wait.

I want to try to give you some responses to some of these most common excuses that we have been talking about. They may not work in every situation but can work in many and will give you a feel of how to respond in a positive and constructive way that helps you to get paid.

If a customer tells you that they don't have any money or any money coming in to pay you, some things you might respond with could be:

Consumer debt:

> Do you really mean that you have no money at all? If this is a consumer debt, talk to them about community help programs they may be eligible for.
>
> Have you applied for unemployment benefits? When will you get your first check?
>
> I'm sorry to hear that. How are you paying your bills?
>
> Are you looking for a job? Have you applied anywhere? When will you hear back from them? Have you gone on any interviews?

Business debt:

Is it more of a case of cash flow problems? Let them know about training, books or ways they can collect from their past due accounts, or give them a referral to use your collection agency.

What are you going to do? What is the plan? Will you apply for unemployment, sell everything and move in with parents, get a new job?

How much are you short? Once they give you a figure you can work on offering a payment plan and get a payment for the amount they do have on hand.

Have you asked the bank for a loan?

What steps are you considering to resolve this situation?

What is the status of your business right now?

The next objection is when a customer tells you not to worry you will be paid or asks you why you are calling them, saying you don't trust them.

Responses for consumer debt:

It's not a question of trust; we just need to be paid for the product you are already using.

We are not worried about being paid eventually; we are worried about being paid on time.

You trusted us to ship you the product on time at the right price and we did that. By paying us on time you are returning that trust.

Business debt:

Because payment is expected on time we factor that into our pricing. Because of that our pricing saves you money and we feel it is only fair that we are paid on time.

> I know you understand we need you to pay us so we can pay our bills. But we can't be your bank.
>
> Debtor excuse: The check is in the mail

Consumer and business debt:

> Great! When did you mail it? Where did you mail it, to what address, how much was it for? What is the check number?

If the date they give you was too long ago, ask for a new check now over the phone. Let them know that you will return the first check to them if it arrives at your office. This is also a good time to make sure the check is for the full amount due and not a partial payment. I say this based on my experience of learning that you must ask this question. When I first started out collecting I did not ask that question and more than once would receive a check as they had stated but it was for a much smaller amount than what was due. This becomes very frustrating, so be sure to ask the question and verify that the check amount is for the full balance due.

If someone gives you the objection that the product was not as promised or not what they had wanted or the wrong size or any type of problem with the service or merchandise some responses could be:

I wish you had notified us of this before the invoice became past due. Why haven't you contacted us about this?

What exactly is wrong with the service/product? Once they tell you the problem, let them know you will look into it right away and call them back. Go find out where the problem lies and get it resolved or come up with a resolution so you can call the customer back. If the claim is unjustified, some of the things you could say are:

> I carefully reviewed your account and we show that you ordered product # and we shipped product # exactly as you had ordered it.
> OR
> I carefully reviewed your account and we show that product # are $3.00 each and with your discount, we charge you $2.48 each, which is also reflected on your PO#1234.

If you can provide me with something to show you did not order part#, which is on your PO#, and was shipped to you on bill #, we can investigate this further.

One of the most common excuses is to be told that someone never received the invoice or the bill in the mail. Some things you could reply with could be:

We mailed you an invoice inside the package that held your order; did you receive your order?

We sent you an invoice and several statements, let me verify your mailing address and send you another right now.

I sent the invoice to your attention and assumed you had received it by now. Can you mail a check for the full amount today?

Find out if you can have the invoice delivered by messenger and ask them to have a check waiting for the messenger.

We mailed the invoice to – repeat their mailing address – which is the same address we have been mailing invoices to you for 5 years, has your address changed recently? (insert how many years you have been using that address)

If it is a local customer, send someone or tell them you will be right over or stop by on your lunch break and pick it up. I have done this successfully and have found in most cases if they know when you are coming they will leave the check with the cashier or front office and be out to lunch or avoid seeing you. This still works and you get paid and it does cut down on problems with the customer in the future. It has been my experience that once you do this they really don't want you to do it again and so they avoid this situation by paying on time.

Working in business to business collections you know that a common excuse is that the purchase order and the invoice don't match up. If this happens to you ask them:

What exactly doesn't match?

If it is an error on your end, fix it and call them back to let them know it was a mistake and that you have corrected it. Send an invoice and give them short terms to pay it. Call them a few days after mailing the invoice just to make sure they received it, as a customer service call not a collection call.

If it is something that doesn't match that is minor and insignificant tell them you can send a corrected invoice but in the meantime can they process it for payment?

Another favourite excuse or stall tactic is I'm not sure, I will have to check my records and get back to you, or my husband has the check book and he isn't home.

If the debtor is someone you have done business with for years and have never been a problem before and they tell you this, give them the time to check their records but give them a specific date and time that you will call back for the update. If this is a customer or debtor that pays late often and you may have had to call before, make a specific date and time to call back and ask them if they will be there to take your call at that time on that date.

You can also ask what exactly they have to check in their records and let them know the invoice numbers, amounts due, total balance and ask what else they need. Offer to have someone stop by and pick up the check.

In a down economy more businesses have to make collection calls and more people have a harder time paying their bills. If a business account tells you they can't pay you because their customers aren't paying them, there are some things you can do. I have had this happen to me when I was making collection calls and it can be turned into a win-win situation for you and your customer by offering help to them in collecting their receivables. If a customer tells you they can't pay you because their customers don't pay them, you could reply with:

Are your customers not paying you or just paying you slower?

Which customers, all of them, bigger customers?

What are you doing to collect from them?

Have you looked into a bank loan?

What exactly is the problem, maybe I can help.

At least some of your customers are still paying you, can you send me $100 today?

You can also offer suggestions to educational debt collection information you may have used and tell them it helped you. Let them know how you got out of the same situation. If they can relate to you in this way, you increase your chance of getting paid before someone who can't relate.

Sales and Credit departments seem to clash everywhere I have worked. The sales department wants to sell as much as they can but then the credit department is left trying to collect if they oversell and the customer can't pay. I have had customers tell me that their salesman told them not to worry about the past due balance when I called. If that happens to you, you could say:

Who is your sales representative?

When did he/she tell you this?

What exactly did they tell you?

You can also let them know that the salesman has no authority over changing their payment terms, explain to them that they signed a credit application or contract, they received the product or service and the invoice with the terms of sale clearly printed on them. Can I take your payment now over the phone?

If you get the response that the person you need to talk to is not in, you could say:

Could I speak to her supervisor/assistant/the owner of the company?

Who else can I speak to about this right now?

I left a message earlier and yesterday, I haven't had a call back and I can't keep extending the due date on this invoice. Can you please have her call me within the next hour or two because I have to discuss this with my supervisor later?

Another common response to your call is that the person who handles that is not in or they tell you the book keeper or accountant handles that. If you get this response ask for the name of the book keeper and their direct line or extension, ask if the book keeper is the one who issues the checks. Ask to be transferred but only after getting the name and direct number so that if you are disconnected you can call back.

If you call a customer and are told they are deceased offer your condolences and ask if you should call back in a few days or if they can talk now. You can wait until the next call or start with some questions during this call depending on how upset the person on the phone is.

Who should I speak to at this point? This could be an attorney, a family member or another person. When you do speak to whoever is handling the deceased estate you will want to make sure to have the full name and address of the estates administrator, the status of the estate, the names of anyone running a business if there was a business involved, details on any insurance policy.

If you call a customer and they can't help you because the computer is down ask them:

> How long before it is back up?
>
> When is the next check run scheduled? If they don't know or can't check ask them to write you a manual check.

CHAPTER EIGHT

WHAT TO AVOID WHEN MAKING COLLECTION CALLS

I mentioned earlier that making debt collection calls should be treated as a customer service call. If you start making your collection calls with the mindset that they are customer service calls to resolve someone's account, you will be entering into the call with a positive attitude which can only help the situation.

Whenever you call any customer, no matter why you are calling, there are things you should never say. Always treat the customer how you would like to be treated if you were in the same situation. Your job is to get paid not alienate a customer who will then bad mouth your company all over town.

Making debt collection calls is a hard job; most people don't do it because it is their lifelong dream. If you are going to start calling people about debts as part of your job or as your primary job, you need to understand all aspects so that you can be effective without getting worn down. Making collection calls can be a thankless job and you need to have some protection. The most important thing to remember is that this is your job, you are doing a job, there is nothing personal going on, don't read into phone calls or get pulled into an emotionally charged conversation, let it go and move on to the next call.

Since this is a high stress job, you need to be able to relax, get up and walk around and stretch, and leave your job at the office. Clearing your head is crucial to being a good bill collector. We all see the news programs playing the recordings of a threatening message a bill collector is leaving for a debtor, but we never hear the threatening messages that debtors leave for bill collectors. I have been threatened many times on the phone and in person, I have had to have a police escort to my car after work at night due to threats. I have had to have irate customers removed from my office.

Don't take threats lightly and take precautions for your physical safety as well as your mental sanity.

Making collection calls is emotionally draining. Mix it up with breaks, walks and doing something else for a little while if you have a particularly stressful call, then move on.

When you are making collection calls something else to avoid is having any questions about the collection laws where you are collecting. Have a copy of the laws on your desk and study them and know them inside and out. The best way to be effective when making collection calls is to know your stuff.

The top things to avoid when you are ready to make debt collection calls are important; knowing what they are so that you can avoid them will only make you a better collector. Always make sure you are calling at appropriate or allowed times, be conscious of the times zone where you are calling.

Avoid not being prepared, take a look at the customer's account before you call and make sure you understand the notes and know what is going on with the account so you can make a direct call for action. In my experience a call can be derailed when you are not prepared and the customer has a more current update on their account than you do and you end up having to hang up, look into it further and then get back to them.

Avoid being too easy, that is avoid letting the debtor talk you into allowing them to pay a minimal amount with no firm schedule of payment for the entire past due amount. For example, a debtor may tell you what financial problems they have run into which has caused them to become past due with you. Then they may tell you that all they can do is send you $20 now and they don't know when they can pay more. Some collectors just say OK at this point and hang up. This is behaviour to avoid, keep talking to the customer to find out more about their finances, when they get paid, and ask for more than what they offer and set up firm payments for the balance. For example, they will send you $50 today, then $50 every Friday for 1 month at which time you will call them to re-evaluate their financial situation and hopefully raise the payment. I have done this many times with success. The first call when you set up the payments, usually goes pretty well and the customer agrees to everything. When I would hang up with them, I would send them a letter outlining each payment and when it was due, I was very specific including the dates and new balance. Getting the second payment isn't always as easy, and you may get each one but with a little work and follow up, when you try to re-negotiate the amount of the payment after that one month period, that is when I would run into resistance. Another thing that worked for me in this situation was to come back after the second payment or when I was calling about the second payment and offer to lower the payment by $10. Many times that is all it took for the customer to start making the payment regularly without me having to call and spend time and money trying to get them to pay. Sometimes people have a hard time coming up with a certain amount but if you just lower it a little it can be more realistic for them and help you both out.

Avoid missing a payment over the phone opportunity. Getting paid over the phone right away is always better than waiting for a check. I have seen collectors avoid even mentioning accepting a payment over the phone or online and when I have asked them about it, they wave their hand and say, "Oh that's ok; they are just sending a check". No, that is not ok, if you can get payment over the phone and resolve that account right now, you need to do that. To do this make sure you are aware of the many different payment options your business offers. You can accept credit or debit card payments, checks over the phone, maybe a way to pay online using a credit or debit card or PayPal type services. Many customers prefer to pay online so make sure this option is available to them and is easy for them to use. You will thank yourself.

The biggest thing to avoid when making collection calls is losing your emotional side during the call. Making collection calls can be emotionally draining, some of the emotions you will feel when making collection calls include boredom, when someone is going on and on about their life, their finances and why they can't pay you. Annoyance and Frustration with follow up calls to customers who don't seem to be taking this situation seriously. Sadness when you talk to a customer who is in a particularly sensitive situation from death, divorce, loss of home, job or income. Anger when a customer flat out lies to you, again. Extreme anger when a customer acts like a jerk, is demeaning, yells at you or swears at you and calls you names. Exasperation when you take a payment over the phone only to hang up and find the check won't clear, or is a closed account or the credit card is denied. As the collector it is up to you to have compassion and understanding but to remember the goal of your call and stay focused. You can be sorry for someone's situation and offer help but ultimately you are calling to help them find a way to pay you.

As you talk on the phone avoid mumbling and avoid not smiling, a smile can be heard in your voice. This is a small easy thing that you can do that will help you be a better collector. Avoid slumping over your computer looking at customer accounts, and mumbling into your phone. Speak up, you don't want to make this call, the person on the other end doesn't want to talk about this, be clear so you can get through the call and move on. Don't be so unclear or talk too softly so that you have to repeat yourself.

When someone is telling you their story and maybe going on a bit, don't get distracted and stop paying attention or check your email or do anything else. When I was in that situation I would start trying to think of things to say to get back to setting up payments, talking about something they said about a job or borrowing money. Many times a debtor will cry and vent and still be nice on the phone and promise a payment that never comes.

CHAPTER NINE

REALISTIC PAYMENT PLANS

If someone owes you money, they probably owe others money and whoever takes action first or offers a solution first, will get paid first.

It is important to identify which accounts need payment arrangements and contacting those customers before they become overdue. This will dramatically affect the bottom line of your business. Identifying and working with these customers will maximize your cash flow. If you can identify these customers before your competition does, you can be paid before the competition even knows that these customers are even in financial trouble.

You need to create positive steps you can utilize to keep your existing customers, get paid and stay in business. Some tools that you need to do this include offering payment arrangements, procedures and actions that are clearly outlined so that when someone cannot pay nor has a problem paying you know what to do immediately and can take steps to help that customer and help yourself.

If someone is not working they might have other sources of income to pay off debts. They may have credit cards they can use to tide them over until they get a job. During this credit crisis, the advice for working folks is to STOP using their credit cards but if your customer is not working but maybe collecting unemployment, this may be an avenue that is open to them when they don't have many other options. Once they do get a job and have a regular income they can stop using their credit cards and pay them off as quickly as possible. You can also suggest they visit a reputable credit counseling service in their area for help. Keep in mind when people receive lump sums of money anytime during the year, such as a tax return, Christmas club money, a settlement, or vacation pay.

You only need to set up payment arrangements if a customer cannot make payment in full. You must always make the arrangement by talking with the customer, and then you MUST follow up by sending a written notice or letter reiterating what that arrangement is. The only way to make this work is to be very specific. The first line of your letter should say something like, "As per our conversation today and put the date of the call" then go on to state the terms you agreed to, the total due, the number of payments, the due date of each payment and the amount of each payment, I cannot stress enough that you need to be very specific. Also, include a payment envelope if you can, because the easier you make it for the customer to pay, the better your chances are of getting paid.

Never start a call with a customer by asking them how much they can pay; this is just setting you up for failure. To be in control of the call you must let the customer know how much you can accept not the other way around. Once you ask the debtor how much they can pay, you lose all negotiations and you lose control of the call and the situation.

Some of you are new to setting up payment arrangements or might even be new to calling the customers. It is essential to communicate confidence when you are speaking to past due customers. You must be relaxed, confident, and prepared. Remember, everything you do represents your company. Some things to consider when speaking to customers and making payments arrangements:

First impressions – When your customer realizes you are calling about a past due invoice, they will not be happy. You must portray confidence, smile when you speak into the phone, it will be noticeable in your voice.

Your voice should be loud enough to be heard and sound confident, not too loud but not too soft. You want your customer to hear you and understand everything you are saying. Sit up straight in your chair and imagine this person is sitting across from you.

Maintain "eye contact" by staying focused on the call. Don't check your email or watch the other people in your office. Stay focused.

Relax! Sit up straight in your chair; don't play with paperclips or pens on your desk. Use your face, voice, and posture to send your confidence over the phone and in person.

If you put these techniques into effect, you will collect more money and have better results from the calls you make. Take steps to ensure you make your calls in the most effective way the first time, so you don't have to continue to make calls to people that you let have control of the situation.

When deciding how to set up each customer on their specific payment plan, decide how many monthly payments you can extend to the customer, and then divide the total amount due by the number of months you want the balance to be paid in. This will be the monthly payment.

Make sure when you set up a payment arrangement with any customer that you put it in writing. This is very important. Let the customer know that if they cannot make a payment, to call you and let you know, don't just skip the payment because this could void the payment agreement. This way you will keep the lines of communication open with your customer, while helping them to stay on track and keeping some cash flow through your business.

The most important reason you want to offer payment arrangements is to get paid. In this troubled economy it is unrealistic to think your customers can all pay you in full, if a customer is avoiding you or becoming more and more delinquent, it is likely they just cannot pay the entire bill and don't realize they have the opportunity to set up a payment plan. In my years of doing collection work, many of the debtors I would call did not pay because they thought they had to pay the whole amount, Once they realized they could set up a payment plan, they were relieved and open to setting something up to get their bill paid. The key in offering payment arrangements, especially now, is to be realistic.

If you treat your customers well, they will continue to be your customer, they will appreciate that you worked with them and hopefully continue to be loyal and tell others about your business.

Many business owners don't set precedence on payment plans, they accept whatever their customer offers without any negotiation, this is a huge mistake that can cost you the customer, money or your business. Business owners need to maximize their in-house receivables, they cannot get a handle on their receivables without assessing the situation and negotiating a payment plan that works for them, the customer and that is beneficial to all involved.

You have to make payment arrangements that are worth your while, while making the arrangement do-able for the customer. If you set up a blanket payment arrangement, for example, everyone pays $100 a month, if a debtor cannot pay that, you will not get paid. If you work with the debtor and assess their specific situation and agree on $25 every other week, and the customer can do that, you will get paid.

Some tips to help you deal with customers who may need payment plans:

Keep an eye on your accounts receivables and credit limits.
Send your bill upon completion of the work, don't wait 30 days.
Offer more payment options.
Make collection calls and set up any payment plans with someone with authority, not an assistant or clerk.
Be persistent and follow up.
Hold orders until balances have been paid.
Communicate!

If a customer suddenly comes into a lump sum of money you may want to offer a settlement amount rather than payment arrangements. This way the customer pays off the debt for a lesser amount but in one lump sum, so you get a bigger payment all at once. You will have to decide if you can afford to write off any portion of the debt, such as late fees, interest or shipping charges or anything else, then offer the customer a lump sum settlement payment and give it a due date. If they can't pay the settlement amount in one lump sum by the specified date, the offer is void. I have done this with great success; something to look for is when people get their tax returns, Christmas club checks, or a severance package from work. If they can't afford a settlement payment, go back to setting up a payment plan, but explain to them that the payment plan is on the entire balance due, they only get the lesser balance due if they can make the settlement payment in full by a certain date. As with any payment plan or settlement offer, put it in writing.

Specific steps you can take for successful payment arrangements:

Ask for payment in full.
If the customer cannot pay in full, offer to split the balance due into two payments.
If that is not possible, it is time to negotiate by gathering more information on the customers' financial status.

Ask open ended questions so you can evaluate the situation.
Suggest weekly or bi-monthly payments, as opposed to the common monthly payments.
Come to an agreement that is beneficial to you and the customer.
Get a commitment and document it.
Send the customer a letter reiterating your understanding of the agreement.
Ask for a signature on the agreement.

Always start off asking for the payment in full, then go down from there. Always aim high, such as first asking for 100% then 80% then 75% etc. If you leave it up to the customer they will offer the lowest possible amount and that may not help you in your situation at all and certainly won't help them. Based on the economy and how it stands now, you may have to get some pretty small payments but try to get as much as you can as frequently as you can.

Send a confirmation letter the day you make the payment arrangement with the customer.

Send a payment reminder 10 days before the payment is due.

On the due date if you do not have payment, send a letter giving them 5 days to pay before the arrangement is revoked and they go back to full collections on the full amount.

Another example might be that once you have the owner of the business or the debtor on the phone, identify yourself and your company and state the purpose of your call. If the person tells you they cannot pay anything, listen to them and ask specific questions to help you offer a solution to the debtor.

You might ask things such as:

Do you have a job?
Does your spouse have a job?
Are you collecting unemployment?
When do you get paid?

Learn as much as you can about their financial situation and their other bills so you can help to offer a realistic payment plan. If your payment plan is not realistic, it will not happen.

Send a confirmation letter that day, confirming your conversation and the date as well as all payment details. Include how much will be paid on which date and in how many payments, you might want to include what will happen if the arrangements are not met. Offer to re-evaluate their payment arrangement if their financial situation changes.

Anyone who is trying to collect money, even if the amount was agreed upon at the time of the sale, needs to know how to negotiate. Some skills needed to be a good negotiator:

Understanding the negotiation process – highly effective collectors recognize that negotiations are a process. It requires an understanding of the billing, credit approval and payment processes.

Focusing on a Win-Win situation – Win-win means that both parties feel like they have "won" during the collection process. Great bill collectors' help their customers try to solve problems and look for opportunities to make that possible. They also know when to be firm and limit what they do in order to reach an agreement that is acceptable for both parties.

Patience – Too many collectors try to go for the "quick fix" so they can get paid and move on to the next account. Good bill collectors know that patience is a virtue and that rushing the collection process only leads to not getting paid. Gather information BEFORE contacting your customer, then think carefully about possible solutions and this is really critical because major mistakes can be made when you rush.

Confidence – Good collectors are confident when making a call or writing a letter. They aren't arrogant, rude or cocky, they are confident and helpful. You must believe in your ability to reach a win-win agreement with the customer, this is obtained through experience.

Listening skills – People will tell you just about everything you need to know if you ask the right questions or keep quiet long enough for them to continue speaking. The biggest mistake a bill collector can make is not listening or bigger yet, interrupting a customer when that might mean if they had just listened longer, they may have received key information that would assist them in their collection effort. When you call a customer and you state the reason for your call or ask a question, wait for the answer. No matter how long the pause may be, let the customer break that silence with an answer.

Some other skills needed to be able to work with your customers to get paid, or set up payment arrangements are:

Managing the emotional side – customers will get upset that you are calling them. They have bigger and better things to think about other than your bill, they will cry, yell at you, hang up on you and swear at you. When a customer starts to tell you their life history and how this affects how they pay you, you need to be able to have some compassion but offer a solution to get the bill paid. This is when you would offer a payment plan or different payment options.

Prepare a pre-call plan: before you ever call a customer about their balance, you need to research their account. Before you dial, make sure you know the invoice number, date, amount that is past due, how past due it is, the payment history, details of the order and if there were any disputed items. When the customer asks you any question, you need to answer immediately whenever possible, otherwise you lose time and time is money.

Having an opening statement ready – your opening statement should be very brief and to the point. You need to identify yourself and your company, state why you are calling and what you want.

For example:

> "Hi, this is Michelle from KTM Auto calling about your past due balance of $500.00 on invoice #1234 dated 4/1/08. I am calling today to take your payment over the phone to clear this balance from your account. Would you like to pay with a credit or debit card or check by phone?"

STOP

WAIT for an answer and always assume the debtor will pay. This is the point where they may tell you they can't pay in full and you would proceed to start setting up a payment plan.

Ask questions – asking questions with precision and making the transition to the payment arrangement – all your questions should be clear and to the point with silence after each question, so the customer can answer. Make sure you LISTEN.

For example:

> Customer: I can't pay, I don't have any money.
> You: Are you working?
> Customer: Yes, but I just started a job and don't get paid for 2 weeks.
> You: What day will you get paid?
> Customer: Friday
> You: Okay, we can accept a payment of half the balance on Saturday.

This can go on and on, the customer might then tell you they can't pay half, you work down from there until you reach a realistic agreement. Then send out a confirmation letter with all the details of the agreement. Then you call on Friday to remind them about making that payment.

For example:

> "Hi this is Michelle from KTM Auto calling to confirm you will be mailing your check for $50 tomorrow, Saturday as we agreed."

When you start negotiating payment arrangements you are entering into another business agreement with your customer. Some companies write up contracts for payment plans that the customer signs.

Anyone working with your customers to set up payment arrangements needs to:

> Be interested in people, and be a good communicator both verbally and in writing.
> Be persuasive and persistent, with the sensitivity to deal fairly with people in often difficult situations.
> Be able to stay calm under pressure, and be adaptable in sometimes tricky situations.
> Have strong negotiation skills and the ability to explain financial matters firmly and clearly.
> Have mathematical ability to explain payments, financial terms and credit services and policies.

Be able to understand relevant legislation concerning data protection and harassment.
Have office administration and computer skills.

I have outlined the main elements or steps of a payment plan here for you:

Contact is made with the customer.
You ask for payment in full, the customer lets you know that is not possible and asks for a payment plan.
You ask the debtor basic questions regarding their finances
Are you working?
Is your spouse/significant other/roommate working?
When do you get paid?
What other debts do you have to pay? (Credit cards, car payments, day care etc.)
Are you receiving unemployment?
How are you paying your bills now?
What is your profession or what do you do?
How much do you make an hour or week?

Ask questions that will help you to determine the approximate disposable income of the customer.

Depending on the amount of income the customer has and the amount owed, make a realistic estimate on what you would like to ask for in terms of monthly, weekly, bi-weekly etc, payments.

Offer more than one option to the customer so they have a part in the decision which means they are more likely to make those payments.

When a customer that has been set up on a payment plan misses a payment, call them immediately. Let them know you need the payment right then over the phone or the account will go back to the collection department, and further action may be taken. Further action could be, reporting to the credit bureau, putting their account on hold, revoking their credit all together, placing them with an outside collection agency or maybe small claims court. Remember that whatever you tell the customer you "might" do, if they do not follow through with the payment, you must take those actions. Never threaten something you don't intend to follow through on. You will lose all credibility and all chances of getting paid.

When you set up the initial payment arrangement, you would have sent them something in writing, hopefully your document also let them know that if they missed a payment or a payment was late that the payment arrangement would become null and void and the total balance would now be due. Most times that is enough to keep someone on track, especially if they know they cannot come up with the full balance to pay in full. Keeping on top of customers that you set up on payment arrangements is very important, you must become their babysitter and keep them on track.

Letting the customer know you care about their account and their situation enough to work with them to help them to get their bill paid is one of the top methods to improve your payment plans and collections. Another top method for improving your payment plan is to offer the customer something that they perceive as "special treatment" for example, can you write off some interest, or late fees, or lower their interest rate for 3 or 6 months? This gives them some confidence that as they pay their balance is actually going down, and not going up with interest. Another method might be offering to void the final payment if all other payments are made on time. Offering incentives has a huge impact on how you are paid. You may be able to offer something such as suspending all collection calls or activity on the account during the time of the payment plan. Offer many different ways to pay, money orders, western union, checks, credit card, debit card, online payment options, or in person. You can also get the checks up front; say you set up a customer for make 6 monthly payments of $25.00. Have them send you the 6 checks, each one dated for the month it is due.

Remember to:

Work with the customer.
Offer "special treatment".
Offer incentives.
Suspend collection activity as they make payments.
Offer many payment options.
Get checks up front.

If you do everything you just learned about setting up payment arrangements and then skip this step, you may not get paid. Following up with the customers that you give special payment arrangements too is critical to your success and to your getting paid. Many customers will be very agreeable on the phone when you are setting up a payment plan, but once they hang up they forget all about it. This is why it is imperative that you send the agreement in writing immediately after speaking to them, and monitor their account to make sure they are making the payments as agreed.

It is a lot like babysitting, but if you don't do it, you may not get paid at all. Stay on top of your payment plan accounts by printing out aging reports weekly or setting up a tickler file so you know when to contact a customer that is not making their payments as agreed. If you told your customers that if they missed a payment the agreement would be null and void, follow through with that or you will never have any credibility or leverage with that customer again.

Sometimes offering an incentive such as if you make all of the payments on time or early, we will waive the last payment, will keep customers on track.

Another good follow up tool is to send a letter or notice each time you receive a payment, that start out with "Thank you for your payment of $25.00, your new balance is $150.00 and your next payment is due Friday, march 20, 2009. I have enclosed a payment envelope for your next payment."

Stay on top of it and you increase your chances for success. This may seem like a lot of work on your part, but if you don't put the effort in, you will not get paid.

CHAPTER TEN

TOP CLUES YOUR CUSTOMER IS NOT GOING TO PAY YOU

When the economy is thriving business owners aren't as concerned with their accounts receivables because the money may be flowing but unlike the good times, during the tough times you need to really take a look at the people you extend credit to or have extended credit to. Customers that may have always paid you on time can suddenly be faced with trying economic times causing them to be unable to pay you even though they had every intention of paying you.

One of the things to look for are the people who have always paid on time and now are falling behind and watch out for the people who just try to take advantage of the situation to get out of paying you.

You can keep bad debts to a minimum and have more success recovering them if you identify them early. Your actions at this point of your credit-collection procedures are vital. Your reaction can mean the difference between recovery and loss. When you identify a potential bad debt, you need to act promptly and decisively. Usually the more time that passes, the less consumers pay.

Accounts that are carried indefinitely usually originate with creditors who do a limited amount of business, have the highest credit losses or the lowest debt recovery. Most national associations keep track of averages of delinquency for their industry.

You should have a standard, in-house written policy on handling accounts. The policy should include when to call new customers, when to call established customers and when to send letters. It is up to you unless you hire a credit manager, to make sure the policy is followed and kept up to date. Your policy should change as you grow or add new products or services to your inventory, or if you just want to make more money by having a stricter policy and including discounts and other payment incentives.

Assuming that there is regular account billing, you will find that most credit users will pay as agreed. A certain number will pay after a mild reminder. Some will encounter a change in their economic situation that suddenly or gradually makes it difficult for them to pay, such as an illness, accident or loss of job. After a regular follow-up with these consumers, they will usually give insight into their financial situation, their reason for nonpayment, a promise to pay and eventually they will fulfill this promise. A small number of consumers, will require more attention, but will eventually pay.

In order to keep the account good, you must give each account proper and constant attention. It is up to you to start and keep the communication about your payments terms and credit policies open and ongoing with your customer. It is important that your customer know your payment terms and credit policy before they start doing business with you. If communication slows down or stops completely that is a clue that your customer is avoiding you because they know they owe you money and they can't pay. That is your cue to start working on communication, talking about the bill and offering a solution to get it paid. You want to do this as soon as you realize this is happening, because if this customer owes you money he also owes others money and you want to be first in line to get paid.

If you notice that a regular customer has suddenly stopped placing regular orders and is paying slowly that is a clue that they may be having financial problems. When you look at your accounts receivable listing, check for customers who are new to your list, customers that have a balance due in the 30 day, 60 day and 90 day column, customers with a last pay date of over a year ago and a balance over 120 days old. These are all clues that you can use to your advantage to get paid on a debt when many others may not. Also keep an eye out if a regular customer starts placing much smaller orders or is ordering less quantity less often.

I did this when I worked at Rochester Shoe Tree Company. I was the credit manager there and working with Macy's trying to get old invoices paid off and get their account current. They ended up filing for bankruptcy, but because I was aware of that fact almost a year and a half ahead of time, I was able to get their bill paid off before the filing, making

Rochester Shoe Tree very happy and Macy's happy since they restructured and remained a customer. The reason I knew about the filing was because I had been talking to accounts payable for months working on clearing up old balances, getting proof of delivery, working on credit memos and cleaning up their account. I was communicating with them, and I dealt with one person who eventually felt very comfortable talking with me and working with me. That is why sometimes if you have some big accounts it is beneficial to have one person assigned to those accounts that always deals with the same person so they can build a rapport and freely communicate.

Some other things to keep an eye and an ear out for that are clues your customer is going to run into trouble trying to pay your bill include unexpected medical bills, someone new to dealing with a budget or finances that seems confused or frazzled, unemployment, emergencies, separation, divorce or marital problems and the death of a spouse or family member.

In conclusion I would like to just re-cap and repeat some of the most important things you can do to be successful with your credit and collections.

Every single business should have a credit policy. If your business doesn't have a credit policy, you are losing money, sales and not pushing your business to be the best it can be.

Remember making a collection call is completing the sale. The sale is not complete until the bill has been paid.

I have written many credit policies for many different businesses, large and small, retail and service, and have helped them all to make more money. When people hear this they ask me, "What can your books do for me and who needs these books?"

1. Anyone who wants to start their own business.
2. Driven and ambitious people who like to see the results of their work.
3. Business owners who have money owed to them.
4. Business owners who do not have a credit policy for their business.

5. Entrepreneurs who want to be their own boss and make their own future.

My books will help you collect money from your customers in a fast and effective way. I will help you see the actual results of your work, reflected in your bottom line. You will have visible results, collect more money and be more successful when you use my books to help you succeed. You will learn how to weed out and fire slow or non-paying customers that are dragging you and your business down.

MANY people have used my books to make more money, more sales and be more successful. Check out my Credit & Collections Blog for many success stories from people just like you.

Now for the most popular question I am asked the most often….drum roll please….

"How do I create a credit policy and why do I need one?"

A credit policy falls into the same category as a business plan or a marketing plan. If you don't have a business plan, you will not be able to get a loan to start your business. If you don't have a marketing plan, you will not have the media exposure or get the word out about your business. If you don't have a credit policy, you will not be in control of your cash flow or the success of your business.

When you create a credit policy for your business, you should include the plan in your business plan, just as you include your marketing plan. The bank that you approach for a loan will see that you have done your research and that you are very serious about your business, how it will be run and how you will be making money to pay them back. When you include your credit policy in your business plan you have a MUCH better chance of being approved for a loan.

One important thing to remember is that every credit policy is different, just like every business plan or marketing plan is different. It is based on what you want for your business, and how much money you want to make. Your credit policy has to reflect your customer service procedures, your product and how you want your cash to flow. There are so many things to know when you create your policy, including the laws in your state and the states you will be doing business in.

Some business owners have had their business for months or even years and when I give talks about credit policies, credit limits, and credit applications, they say, "I never did any of that and I have so many customers that owe me money and are past due." Many think it is too late to do anything about it, or they are afraid to ask a customer for the money or ask them to fill out a credit application. They think they will make the customer mad and lose the business. If the customer is past due or not paying you, why do you worry about alienating them? This is a customer you do not need.

If someone is not paying you, they are not helping you. Wouldn't you rather have a customer that pays you? Stop working for free.

If you have customers that owe you money right now, today, you can and should do something about it immediately! Add up how much money is past due or is not being paid, the dollar amount will shock you. Now is the time to take action! I am going to list some action tips here that you and every business owners can take today to start making more money by collecting what is owed to you. Do not wait, you are in business to make money, aren't you?

Action Steps to take Today

1. Go through your accounts receivable and find out who owes you money, how much and how many days past due it is. Print this list or put the invoices in a pile.
2. Set aside an hour a day to sit down and call those customers or have someone in your office call them for you.
3. Create a series of collection letters to send out to the customers who are approaching the past due mark or who are 30-60 days past due and who you could not reach on the phone. If you do not have any letters check out one of my letters and forms books for actual letters I have used that are very effective.
4. Mail those letters today!
5. Put a note in your calendar to call those people in 1 week if you do not have their payment, and if you can't reach them by phone on that day, send another letter that same day.
6. Follow up on all phone calls and letters. If you don't do this, don't do anything, follow up is the biggest collection tool you can use.

You worked hard to have your own business and you deserve to get paid. Don't let your customers control your cash flow. Take the above steps and you will see an increase in your collection immediately.

Some other things you can do to gain knowledge or help you with collections are to network with other business owners who are doing the same thing. Take a moment to visit my Credit & Collections Blog or group on LinkedIn called The Guide to Getting Paid or Starting a Collection Agency and you can network, exchange ideas, ask questions and learn more about debt collection starting today.

I get many people who email and ask me questions about credit, debt collection, credit policies and procedures and getting paid and I want to list the top collection errors that I have found businesses do the most. In my 18 years as a bill collector, these stand out the most.

1. No credit policy. – So many business owners do not have a credit policy. How do you expect to get paid if you don't have a credit policy?
2. Extending credit to anyone who walks through the door or calls to place an order. – I personally know of so many business owners that do this. They are so excited to make a sale that they do not check credit, outline terms, or even get any information from the customer. Then when the person doesn't pay, or the check bounces the creditor (you) doesn't know what to do.
3. Receiving NSF or "bad" checks. – This is the most popular yet. I cannot stress this enough, be prepared BEFORE you receive a bad check. Make a sign to hang in your store or post on your website or both. The sign should say:

What you charge when a check is returned.

What will happen to the account if a check is returned?

Avoid more bad checks by having every customer fill out a credit application, and then CHECK THE REFERENCES!

If you only do one thing, get signed credit applications and check the references. This will only cost you a small amount of time and effort and the results will be extraordinary.

When is the last time you tried to apply for a credit card or a loan and didn't have to fill out any paperwork? Your business depends on you to protect it from failing, maintaining cash flow and to be successful. Don't let your business or yourself down.

RESOURCES

Credit and Collections blog www.Credit-and-Collections.com
Michelle Dunn's website www.MichelleDunn.com

Books by Michelle

The Credit Policy Workbook http://www.amazon.com/Credit-Policy-Workbook-step--ebook/dp/B006XGJRZY

The Ultimate Credit and Collections Handbook, the check IS in the mail! http://www.amazon.com/Ultimate-Credit-Collections-Handbook-Michelle/dp/1599180251/

How to Get your Customers to Pay: Fast, Easy, Effective Letters http://michelledunn.com/store?page=shop.product_details&flypage=garden_flypage.tpl&product_id=26&category_id=9

Getting Paid using Social Media in Collections http://www.amazon.com/Getting-Paid-Using-Social-Media/dp/1453759425/

The Guide to Getting Paid, weed out bad paying customers, collect on past due balances, and avoid bad debt. http://www.amazon.com/Guide-Getting-Paid-Customers-Balances/dp/1118011619/

Choosing the Right Collection Agency for your Business http://www.amazon.com/Choosing-Collection-Business-Collecting-ebook/dp/B0078EVD98/

How to help you Get Paid, collection forms and letters http://www.amazon.com/Help-Credit-Collections-Forms-Letters/dp/0970664532/

LinkedIn discussion group, The Guide to Getting Paid: http://www.linkedin.com/groups/Guide-Getting-Paid-2652085

YahooGroups discussion group, Credit and collections: creditandcollections-subscribe@yahoogroups.com

Credit Management Association http://creditmanagementassociation.org/

The Stellar Risk Report & Journal http://www.stellarrisk.com/category/reports-journal/

ABOUT THE AUTHOR

In 1998, when Michelle was getting a divorce and had 2 small children, she started a collection agency from home leaving her full time job 6 months later. Her agency did very well and grew over the next 8 years until Michelle sold it in 2006 to write full time.

Michelle knew what business owners needed and had already written a couple of books that were selling well. "But it was still a huge leap", she says, "I was a single mom with two sons." I started putting together my ideas, set up an office in my home, and used the income from book sales to fund publishing more books.

That same year Michelle self published 4 books and e-books before landing her first book contract with Entrepreneur Press to write *The Ultimate Credit and Collections Handbook, the check IS in the mail*. She then self published a couple more business books before getting a book deal with John Wiley & Sons Publishing for her first hardcover book, *The Guide to Getting Paid, weed out bad paying customers, collect on past due balances, and avoid bad debt.*

Today Michelle Dunn continues to write columns and books and presents webinars & offers consulting, sharing how business owners can limit credit risk in this economy as well as learn how they can prevent some bad debt, and collect from past due customers. To learn more, visit www.MichelleDunn.com and www.Credit-and-Collections.com